To Bailey, my "daughter" in Christ

SHOULD CHRISTIANS ALWAYS OPPOSE WAR?

And 11 Other Difficult Questions Believers Ask

Bill Bouknight

SHOULD CHRISTIANS ALWAYS OPPOSE WAR?

And 11 Other Difficult Questions Believers Ask

WILLIAM R. BOUKNIGHT

Bristol House, Ltd.
2004

SHOULD CHRISTIANS ALWAYS OPPOSE WAR?

And 11 Other Difficult Questions Believers Ask

Published by Bristol House, Ltd.

First Printing, June 2004

ISBN: 1-885224-46-X

Printed in the United States of America.

BRISTOL HOUSE, LTD.
P.O. Box 4020
Anderson, Indiana 46013
Phone: 765-644-0856
Fax: 765-622-1045
To order call: 1-800-451-READ (7323)

TABLE OF CONTENTS

FOREWORD

I live in Germantown, Tennessee, a bedroom community of Memphis. Sometime in 2002 the people in my neighborhood received a specially prepared postcard advertising a series of sermons to be preached by my friend, Dr. Sam Shaw of Germantown Baptist Church. Each of the sermons was introduced by the words "I Have a Friend Who . . ."

I was impressed by Sam's series and, since imitation is the sincerest form of flattery, I decided to develop a similar series of sermons. I spoke to a different series of topics and concerns, but each sermon title included the words "I Have a Friend Who . . . ."

This collection of sermons, which appear as separate chapters here, are my attempts to shine the light of biblical truth on the toughest ethical issues in contemporary American culture. In each one I allow the Bible to converse with "my friend" about one particular subject. Each subject is controversial and volatile. Often the biblical position that I champion is different from the stance taken by "my friend." But the very fact that the conversation is between friends gives it a respectful and kindly tone. I hope such dialogue creates more light than heat.

I offer heartfelt thanks to the wonderfully responsive people of Christ United Methodist Church in Memphis. They heard these sermons during 2003 and were kind enough to offer their suggestions and reactions. I am privileged to be their senior minister.

Special thanks are in order to Mrs. Anita Jones, the finest secretary a pastor ever had. She worked patiently and conscientiously on this project, helping me translate these sermons into a manuscript suitable for publishing.

The underlying assumption behind these sermons and this book is that the Bible speaks clearly and powerfully to all of the ethical dilemmas of this or any age. There is nothing antiquated or outdated about the Bible. It is still the true rule and guide for faith and practice. When read intelligently and under the influence of the Holy Spirit, it conveys the inspired wisdom of God.

William R. Bouknight
Memphis, Tennessee
October 2003

I Have a Friend Who . . .

BELIEVES THAT FAITH AND SCIENCE ARE ENEMIES

Genesis 1:1, Psalm 19:1–4a

At times faith and science have feuded like the Hatfields and McCoys. Sometimes the church as the protector of faith has been at fault. Poor old Galileo was a seventeenth-century astronomer who discovered that the planets revolve around the sun. The Church was convinced that the sun and all other planets revolved around the earth, though the Bible does not say so. Galileo was tried by the Roman Catholic Inquisition. The vilified scientist spent the final eight years of his life under house arrest. The church was wrong to go beyond the Bible in presenting unproved claims as good science.

Sometimes the fault is with science. The Disney empire, creators of the Epcot Center in Orlando, Florida, displays bad science. They advertise as a fact of science (rather than just theory) that God has nothing to do with the creation of the earth. Instead, they claim that billions of years ago an accidental "Big Bang" caused all we see. Then sometime later several protozoa came crawling up out of the primordial slime. Over the ensuing billions of years they continued to evolve into every known species of life. To believe that two protozoa simply kept reproducing until finally there appeared Jennifer Lopez is a real stretch.

The Epcot Center is bad science because it presents an unproved theory of science as a fact of science, without allowing for the possibility of other theories.

The truth is that *faith and science need not be enemies.* The Christian doctrine of creation by a rational God led scientists to expect a world that was ordered and intelligible. After all, God is a God of order, not chaos. The Bible presents a picture of a loving, dependable God. Such a God could be expected to create a universe of dependable natural laws. That helps the scientist. Can you imagine how much trouble scientists would have if a natural law like gravity worked only occasionally?

Something else about the Christian gospel helps scientists. We believe in God as Creator rather than as part of the created order. We worship God, not his creation. Because early Christians believed that nature was not to be feared or worshiped, it was easier to consider nature as an object of scientific study.

Dr. Peter Hodgson, distinguished scientist at Oxford, declared, "Christianity provided just those beliefs that are essential for science, and the whole moral climate that encouraged its growth."[1]

Perhaps the greatest scientist of all time, Sir Isaac Newton of the seventeenth century, formulated the laws of gravity. He was a devout Christian who wrote both theology and science books.

Having made the point that faith and science need not be enemies, let's consider a loaded question: *Concerning evolution, can faith and science get along?*

First, let's distinguish between microevolution and macroevolution. Microevolution means simply adaptation that goes on over time within a given species. For example, human beings are getting taller. We are gradually losing our wisdom teeth, not because we aren't so wise but because we don't need those teeth so much as the cave men did. Farmers can breed for sweeter corn and faster horses, but they still end up with corn and horses. Most Christians believe in microevolution.

Macroevolution is very different. This is the theory developed by Charles Darwin claiming that naturalistic evolution is the creator of the universe and that God had nothing to do with it. According to this theory, all life developed from a single, original species, and one species can develop into another. For example, an ape can become a man; a fish can become a kangaroo. Macroevolutionists believe that there is only a quantitative rather than a qualitative difference between a human being and an animal.

Christians would have no problem if macroevolution were presented as a theory. We vehemently protest when it is taught as fact. Yet recently the National Association of Biology Teachers released a position statement declaring, "The diversity of life on earth is the outcome of evolution: an unsupervised, impersonal . . . process, governed by natural selection, chance, and changing environments. Creation beliefs have no place in the science classroom."[2]

Unfortunately, this view of evolution is presented to our children at Epcot Center as fact. I would have no problem if in the introduction the narrator said, "What you are about to see is one theory of how the world began. Other theories exist, including the possibility that the universe was created by a higher power."

But no, the macroevolutionists want to take an unproved theory and in a very unscientific way present it as proved fact.

The Bible takes a different view of the origin of the universe. Simply and eloquently, Genesis 1:1 declares: "In the beginning

God created the heavens and the earth." Notice that the Bible assumes God's existence. It never argues about the matter. God had no beginning. In the Old Testament the Hebrew verb for "create" is used only for divine activity, never for human endeavors.

We discover in Genesis 1 that God created the universe in six days. Christians differ in their understanding of how long each day was in the story of creation. Some Christians believe that God did it all in twenty-four-hour days. Other Christians point out that the Hebrew word for "day" has several meanings, one of which is "era." I believe that "era" is the proper interpretation. After all, the sun was not created until the fourth day of creation. Therefore, it was difficult to have a 24-hour day without a sun for the earth to revolve around. If God created the universe over a period of six eras, that leaves plenty of room for the dinosaurs to come and go.

Genesis is not a science book. It does not attempt to answer the "How?" or "When?" questions of creation. Those are science questions. The Bible answers the questions "Who?" and "Why?" Those are theology questions. Who created the universe? God. Why did he do it? Because he is a loving God and wanted to fellowship with human beings as his children. How did trouble, disease and death enter God's world? Blame sin. Why did God allow human beings the option of sin? Because if human beings were not truly free to choose, they would not be truly human.

That brings me to a concluding claim: *faith and science can be friends.* Christianity is all for responsible science. Science may discover more cures for diseases, alternate sources of energy and countless other ways to make life on earth more abundant. In Genesis 1:28, God commanded the human race to subdue the world and have dominion over it. God wants us to eliminate as much misery as possible on this little planet. Science is a powerful tool in making that happen. Consider what the scientists at St. Jude Hospital in Memphis have done in the battle against leukemia.

Not only that, we believe that the more scientists discover, the more evidence they will find for the existence of God, although no one can ever prove God scientifically. But as the psalmist wrote, "The heavens declare the glory of God; the skies proclaim the work of his hands" (Psalm 19:1). St. Paul declared, ". . . since the creation of the world God's invisible qualities—his eternal power and divine nature—have been clearly seen, being understood from what has been made, so that men are without excuse" (Romans 1:20).

The great astronomer Alan Sandage said, "It was my science that drove me to the conclusion that the world is much more complicated than can be explained by science. It is only through the Supernatural that I understand the mystery of existence."[3]

Albert Einstein, *Time*'s Person of the Twentieth Century, said that the universe "reveals an intelligence of such superiority" that it overshadows all human intelligence.[4]

Dr. A. Cressy Morrison, former president of the New York Academy of Sciences, used an interesting example to point to the evidence for God in the universe. He said, "Suppose I take ten pennies and mark each one of them with a number, one through ten. Then I put them in my pocket and give them a good shake. Suppose I tell you that I am going to pull from my pocket penny number one, then put it back, and pull out penny number two, put it back, and then pull out each numbered penny in order through number ten. Do you know what the odds are of my being able to do that? About one chance in ten billion. The odds are even worse than winning the lottery."

Then Dr. Morrison said, "The odds are even greater against this created order being an accident. There is an intelligent Designer behind it all. There has to be."[5]

Just look at the evidence. First, our temperature. The sun is twelve thousand degrees Fahrenheit. We are ninety-three million miles from the sun. That combination is, in Goldilocks' language, just right! If earth's average temperature were fifty degrees hotter or cooler, life would cease to exist.

Or consider the rotation of the earth. Earth rotates 365 times each year as it passes around the sun. Suppose it rotated thirty-six times instead. Our nights and days would be ten times as long. Earth would be unbearably hot on one side and unbearably cold on the other.

Consider our water. When water freezes, it expands and floats. If water did not have this unique capacity, lakes and rivers would freeze all the way to the bottom, and all fish would die.

Or consider the composition of our air. Oxygen constitutes about twenty-one percent of our atmosphere. What if it were fifty percent? Then if someone lighted a match, we'd all go up in flames. Who decided that the oxygen level would be twenty-one percent? Do you really believe it was an accident?

Bishop Lloyd Wilke used to tell about a preacher he knew when he was a teenager. He taught a group of boys each Saturday morning at the church. Afterward he would go into the sanctuary and open the great pulpit Bible to the text he would use the following day. He was an emotional preacher, often pounding the pulpit for emphasis. One Saturday afternoon the boys slipped into the sanctuary and placed a thumbtack under the scriptural page. On the following day the preacher asked the congregation rhetorically, "And who created the world?" and down came his fist for emphasis. Suddenly he jerked back his fist in pain and shouted, "The confounded boys did it."

That preacher believed as we do—if you see enough evidence, you must conclude that there was a planner.

If science and faith have good boundaries and mutual respect, they can be good neighbors. We Christians ought to have enough confidence in God and the Bible not to be threatened by science. Indeed responsible science is our ally.

Science on the other hand ought to discern between an unproved theory and a proved fact. They ought to call evolution what it is—a theory.

We need never worry that science might make faith obsolete. Faith alone can speak to the deepest needs of people, showing them their place in the universe and their relationship to the Creator. Science can never deal with the problems of loneliness, grief or guilt. Only in Christ do we find answers for humanity's deepest needs.

A great scientist, Dr. John Lennox, used a simple example to explain the relationship between faith and science: "Suppose I bring before you the most beautiful cake you have ever seen, and ask the best scientists in the world to analyze it. A nutritionist could tell me the precise ingredients in the cake. A biochemist could tell me about the electrons and protons and the quarks. Then the mathematician could inform me about the equations governing the motions of those electrons, protons, and quarks.

"But no scientist could tell me who made the cake or why he or she made it. Then up would step Aunt Matilda. And she might say, 'I made the cake and the purpose of it is to celebrate my nephew's birthday.'"

No amount of scientific analysis can tell us who created the universe or why it was created, unless the Creator steps up and speaks. That he has done in a book called the Bible and through his Son, Jesus Christ.[6]

Professor James Simpson, who paved the way for painless surgery through anesthetics, was asked, "What was the most important discovery of your life?" He replied, "The most important discovery I ever made was when I discovered Jesus Christ."[7]

Can faith and science get along? Oh yes! Good fences make good neighbors.

ENDNOTES

[1] John Young, *The Case Against Christ* (London: Hodder & Stoughton, 1986).

[2] Cited in Chuck Colson, *Answers to Your Kids' Questions* (Wheaton: Tyndale, 2000), 46.

[3] *The Hand of God,* ed. Michael Reagan (Atlanta: Lionheart, 1999).

[4] Cited in Colson, op.cit., 19.

[5] Cited in Charles R. Swindoll, *Growing Strong in the Seasons of Life,* (Grand Rapids: Zondervan, 1983), 374–75.

[6] Cited in Nicky Gumbel, *Searching Issues,* (Colorado Springs: Cook Ministry Resources, 1996), 98.

[7] Ibid., 93.

QUESTIONS

1. What is troublesome about the way some educators and media present the theory of evolution? Should the theory of evolution be taught at all?
2. Why should Christians encourage and support scientific endeavors rather than boycotting them?
3. Do you think it will ever be possible to prove the existence of God scientifically? Why or why not?
4. Should we worry that science might make our faith obsolete?

5. List some problems that science alone will never solve.
6. What does the author mean by the last sentence in the chapter: “Good fences make good neighbors”? Do you agree or disagree with this statement, and why?
7. In the chapter, the author gives several examples of natural conditions that are perfect for sustaining life, which point to an intentional Creator. Name some other scientific facts about our world that suggest that life is not just an accidental by-product of random occurrences.
8. Should Christian beliefs about Creation be discussed in the classroom? If not, how should the Christian view that God is responsible for creating everything be communicated?

I Have a Friend Who . . .

LIKES JESUS BUT DISLIKES THE CHURCH

MATTHEW 16:13–19; 1 JOHN 4:20–21

Sometimes I think the church needs a good public relations firm. In America and Europe, the church is disparaged, ridiculed and ignored by many. Many people think of church as hard pews, unsingable hymns, enforced silence and excruciating boredom. Abraham Lincoln said, "If all the people who fell asleep in church were laid out end to end . . . they would be a great deal more comfortable."[1]

A little girl became restless as the preacher's sermon dragged on and on. Finally, she leaned over to her mother and whispered, "Mommy, if we give him the money now, will he let us go?"

The image of the clergy has been battered by revelations of sexual abuse and greed. In the movies, preachers fare little better than used-car dealers and morticians. Clergy are usually portrayed as totally naïve or as raving hypocrites.

Some people have high regard for Jesus but don't think too highly of organized religion. You know the most common criticisms leveled against the church—it's boring, hypocritical, irrelevant and obsessed with money. And let's be honest . . . we must plead guilty, to some degree, to all of those charges. Often we preachers turn the most exciting news the world ever heard into something bland and boring. At times our singing sounds like a funeral dirge.

The criticism that hurts most is the charge of hypocrisy. There is a huge gap between the standards of Jesus and the behavior of Christians. The public sees little difference between church members and unchurched folks. Our divorce and abortion rates and our credit ratings are about the same as the unchurched. Going to church does not make you a Christian any more than standing in a garage makes you a car. The sociologist George Barna estimates that half of all adults who attend Protestant churches on a typical Sunday are not Christians.[2] That is, they have never experienced a genuine spiritual rebirth, and are not in a personal relationship with Jesus Christ. But I'm mighty glad such folks are in church, because there is no other place where it is easier for Christ to reach them.

Using Scripture as our source of truth, let's consider four questions about the church. First, *why is the church even necessary? Isn't religion just a one-on-one relationship between a person and God?*

No. Christianity is not just a one-on-one relationship with God. A solitary Christian is a contradiction in terms. Our Methodist founder John Wesley said, "The New Testament knows nothing of solitary religion." There are two things we simply cannot do alone. We cannot marry alone and one cannot be a Christian alone.[3] When any person enters into a personal relationship with Jesus Christ, he or she immediately becomes a part in the body of Christ, a group of Christians called the church. In the letter of First John, we are told that if we don't love our sisters or brothers in the body of Christ, we cannot love God.

The church is not an optional group activity for the Christian; the church is the body of Christ. St. Paul wrote, "Christ is the head of the church, his body, of which he is the Savior" (Ephesians 5:23). So, you see, saying that you love Christ but don't like the church is like saying, "I want to marry Sally but I don't want to live with her." It's a contradiction, an oxymoron.

Before Saul was known as St. Paul, he traveled all over the Middle East persecuting Christians. On the road to Damascus, Saul met the risen Christ. Jesus said to him, "Saul, Saul, why do you persecute me?" (Acts 9:4). Notice that Jesus did not say, "Why are you persecuting my people?" or "Why are you persecuting my church?" No, he said, "Why are you persecuting me?" Isn't it amazing that Jesus Christ would look at a group of sinners like you and me and say, "They are my body"?

So, you see, to say that you like Jesus but don't care for the church is to totally misunderstand who Jesus is. Jesus Christ and his body, the church, are one. Can you imagine saying to a groom on his wedding day, "I think you are a great guy, but your bride is ugly"? He would not appreciate that. Neither does our Lord appreciate someone saying, "I like you but I don't like your bride and your body, the church."

Here is the second question: *Why is the evil one so intent on keeping people out of the local church?*

The Bible declares that we are battling against powerful demonic forces. Whether you call the evil leader "Satan" or "the devil" or "the force," never doubt that we are battling a spiritual enemy intent on destroying our eternal souls. St. Paul taught us that "our struggle is not against flesh and blood, but . . . against the spiritual forces of evil in the heavenly realms" (Ephesians 6:12).

Satan has a simple, three-point strategy: keep people out of church, out of the Bible, and out of prayer. If he can achieve two out of three of those objectives, he will usually win the battle.

Why is Satan so intent on keeping people out of church? Not because he is afraid of preachers. Not because he fears our organizational ability or group psychology. No, Satan hates the church because the Spirit of the living Christ is here in a special way. Jesus said, ". . . where two or three come together in my name, there am I with them" (Matthew 18:20).

The Holy Spirit is everywhere in God's world. But when two or three gather in his name, the presence and power of Jesus are concentrated in an awesome manner. This is the case even if the preaching is bad and the music is worse. Satan despises church because in that fellowship a person is more exposed to Jesus than anywhere else on earth.

Satan, who is the father of all lies, uses all his vaunted salesmanship to keep people out of churches. One of his favorite lies is this one: "You can be a very spiritual person without going to church. In fact, given all the faults of churches, you might be a better Christian outside the church." Don't fall for that lie!

Here is the third question: *What difference has the church made in our world?*

First, the church has been and is the greatest serving institution in history. Arnold Toynbee, the great historian, wrote, "I submit to you that there is no significant institution on earth that did not have its beginning at the altar of the Christian Church." The church has many critics but no rivals in the work of serving humanity. Even as early as the Fourth Century, the church in Rome was feeding nearly twenty thousand of that city's poor. In the church, neurotic folks are cared for rather than ridiculed. Abject failures are offered forgiveness and a second chance. The poor receive special consideration.

Today in most urban ghettos, the church is the only institution left to counter the effects of liquor stores, drug dealers and street hustlers.

One of my favorite waitresses did not report for work one weekend. Her employer was very worried about her. I prayed for her and then dropped by the restaurant on Monday. I was thankful that she had returned. She said to me, "Pastor, an old addiction got hold of me. I spent the weekend gambling in Tunica. But with God's help I will beat this thing yet. I will be at your church this week and every week for the meeting of Gamblers Anonymous."

Occasionally one hears criticism because the church is a tax-exempt organization. I submit to you that if the church were paid even a minimal charge for every meal provided, every scout troop sponsored, every twelve-step group offered, every hour of free counseling and every caring visit to hurting people, no government on earth could afford the church.

A second difference the church has made is this: At her best she has had the courage to stand up for her convictions. I confess that at times we have been slow. It took us much too long to get our hearts right about race relations. But usually the church has fought any government or institution that would steal dignity or freedom from persons. The church gave birth to and reared Martin Luther King, Jr.; the German Lutheran, Dietrich Bonhoeffer, who opposed Hitler; and, more recently, the Reverend John Kaiser, a Roman Catholic priest found alongside a highway in Kenya with a gunshot to the back of the head.

The main reason that the abortion rate is going down in America is because more and more churches are declaring that the unborn baby is not a choice but a baby, a tiny human being made in the image of God.

No wonder the communists hate the church. No wonder Muslim dictators hate the church. At her best she has championed the principles of Christ whatever the costs. I wouldn't give you two cents for an organization whose purpose is to please everybody and offend no one. I have no respect for any institution that is afraid of controversy. I salute the Boy Scouts for continuing to require high moral standards for its scoutmasters, though many people criticized them for it. I love the church because at her best she has had the courage of her convictions.

Of course, the church's greatest work is pointing people to Jesus Christ. Other organizations such as the Rotary, garden clubs, and Chambers of Commerce do good things for the community. But the church alone leads burdened, guilty, mixed-up people to the only One who can lift burdens, save souls and change lives. His name is Jesus. To every worship service come burdened souls whose heart cry is, "Sir, we would like to see Jesus" (John 12:21). It is the church's privilege, through the power of the Holy Spirit, to introduce people to Jesus Christ.

The last question is this: *What are the long-term prospects for the church?* The answer, in teenager terms, is "awesome!" or "out of sight!"

The church is the only institution on earth guaranteed to last forever. How do I know? Because Jesus said so. Our Lord said, ". . . I will build my church, and the gates of Hades [or "hell"] will not overcome it" (Matthew 16:18). The gates of hell are generally considered to mean death. So we have a promise that the church will not die. Then we are told in the book of Revelation that when Jesus returns in glory to close down history, his bride will be waiting on him. Who is his bride? The church! (See Revelation 19:7.)

Just think about it. Few companies, even great ones like FedEx or General Electric or General Motors, last one hundred years. Few nations have survived as long as one thousand years. But the church of Jesus Christ has an eternal guarantee from God.

Today some two billion people call themselves Christians. Christianity is the largest and fastest-growing religion on earth.

The United Methodist Church is growing worldwide at the rate of about one million members per year. By the year 2025, there will be over 2.6 billion Christians, the largest faith group by far, and half of that population will be in Latin America and Africa. The center of Christianity is moving from Europe and North America to Africa, Latin America and Asia.[4]

Every empire that has set out to crush the church has itself been ground to dust. Every philosophy based on the denial of Jesus will ultimately be rejected. Every ideology that ignores Christ finds no enduring truth with which to sustain itself. Gibraltar will crumble before the church goes out of business.

In our Christ United Methodist family in Memphis, there is a lovely little three-year-old girl named Camille. On a recent rainy Sunday morning, several members of her family had the sniffles. Mom and Dad had planned to sleep in. But Camille was up early. Dad got up and met her in the kitchen. He said, "Honey, I'll fix breakfast. What are you hungry for? Cereal, pancakes, waffles, or what?" She looked up at him and said, "I'm hungry for church." That whole family got out of bed, dressed and headed for church. Even little children have a hunger for God and know that the best place to meet him is at church.

If you're a skeptic or a seeker, I dare you to hang around a Bible-believing church. God longs to fill that empty space within you. The Lord is gently knocking on the doors of your heart. In church you are at ground zero of God's grace!

I like the billboard that has appeared in several cities, with this message in huge letters: "MEET ME AT MY HOUSE. (SIGNED) GOD."

ENDNOTES

[1] Nicky Gumbel, *Questions of Life* (Colorado Springs: Cook Ministry Resources, 1996), 217.

[2] George Barna, *Evangelism That Works* (Ventura: Regal, 1995), 38.

[3] Gumbel, op. cit., 223.

[4] Philip Jenkins, "The Christian Century," *Wall Street Journal* (January 3, 2003).

QUESTIONS

1. In addition to those criticisms of the church by the unchurched the author cites at the beginning of this chapter, what other complaints have you heard? Do these accusations have any validity?
2. Why is there such a big gap between what Christians profess to believe and the worldly actions of many who attend church regularly?
3. Why is Christianity *not* a do-it-yourself project? Wouldn't it be easier to follow Christ on our own, without being dragged down by the imperfect folk sitting in the pews?
4. What lies and schemes have you observed Satan using to keep people away from church? Which do you think is the most successful?
5. What difference has the church made in your life? In the lives of people you know?
6. What can the church offer the larger community that even great civic clubs cannot? How is the church different from a nonprofit social service organization?
7. The church seems to be declining in modern times. Will it ever disappear from the face of the earth? Why or why not?

I Have a Friend Who . . .

BELIEVES THAT CHRISTIANS SHOULD ALWAYS OPPOSE WAR

PSALM 46; ROMANS 13:1–4

This sermon was preached at Christ United Methodist Church, Memphis, Tennessee, on February 9, 2003, just a few weeks before the second Persian Gulf War began.

I have a friend who believes that Christians should always oppose war. A similar view was expressed last week in Memphis by Reverend Doctor William Sloane Coffin. Many years ago he was the chaplain at a university where I was a student, so I heard him preach many times. Even as I read his remarks in the newspaper, I thought back twelve years to 1991. At that time Dr. Coffin and many other church leaders urged America not to intervene in the Persian Gulf area. But if America and her allies had not liberated Kuwait and sent Saddam Hussein scurrying back to Baghdad, I wonder what the Middle East would be like today.

Let's look at moral issues relative to a possible war with Iraq, in the light of biblical truth.

First, the pacifist position has always been a respected minority position among Christians. A classic pacifist is one who opposes and will not participate in any violence. Over the last two thousand years many Christians have been pacifists; however, the majority of Christians have not held that view.

It may surprise you to know that Jesus was not a pacifist, at least in the classic sense of opposing all violence. If you had asked the moneychangers in the temple whether Jesus was a pacifist, they would have replied, "Are you kidding? He drove us out with a whip!"

Jesus allowed his disciples to carry swords, and the swords were not for killing snakes. They were for self-defense. At one point Jesus said, "'If you don't have a sword, sell your cloak and buy one.' . . . The disciples said, "See Lord, here are two swords.' 'That is enough,' he replied" (Luke 2:36–38).

At least one of Jesus' disciples was a Zealot. He was part of a group dedicated to the violent overthrow of the Roman Empire.

While Jesus was not a pacifist, a primary thrust of his life and ministry was against violence and war. He said, "Blessed are the peacemakers, for they will be called sons of God" (Matthew 5:9). The United Methodist *Book of Discipline* declares that "war is incompatible with the teachings and example of Christ."[1]

Secondly, *the New Testament ethic for individuals differs from the mandate for national leaders.*

Jesus' famous Sermon on the Mount as recorded in Matthew 5–7 is directed primarily toward individual Christians. Jesus said, "If someone strikes you on the right cheek, turn to him the other also." We Christians, acting as individuals, are not supposed to retaliate. We are supposed to return good for evil.

President Bush as a head of state has a different responsibility spelled out in Romans 13. "He is God's servant, an agent of wrath to bring punishment on the wrongdoer" (Romans 13:4).

The Bible recognizes that if there were no enforcers of justice, chaos would prevail. The national ruler is clearly authorized to use force. The same verse says that ". . . he does not bear the sword for nothing."

As an individual Christian, I am supposed to relate to other individuals with kindness rather than force. But if I am in the United States armed forces, acting under the command of the President, I become his means of delivering justice to the evildoer.

Someone might ask, "Aren't Jesus' standards for individual behavior contradictory to the tasks of the national leader in Romans 13?" The two exist in tension, always reminding us that even when the national leader has to use lethal force, this is not God's *ideal* plan.

A third truth is obvious: *War is always a tragedy.* One of the contributions of Stephen Spielberg's classic World War II movie, *Saving Private Ryan,* was to remind us of the horrors of war. Our veterans know that truth all too well.

Because of the awful suffering brought about by any war, The United Methodist *Book of Discipline* declares that "We deplore war and urge the peaceful settlement of all disputes among nations."[2]

Isaiah revealed God's plan for a world in which "Nation will not take up sword against nation, nor will they train for war anymore" (Isaiah 2:4b). The psalmist saw God working toward the same goal: "He makes wars cease to the ends of the earth; he breaks the bow and shatters the spear, he burns the shields with fire" (Psalm 46:9).

About twenty years ago a layman in the church I was serving was dying of cancer. Shortly before his death, during a pastoral visit, he said, "Pastor, I was a bombardier on a B-29 during World War II. I killed lots of people. If I had to do it over, I would. It was essential that we win that war. But that still does not make it right. I want to confess and ask forgiveness for the necessity of killing all those people." We prayed a prayer together. I was so deeply impressed by this layman who understood that just because something is necessary does not make it good or right. There is no place in Christianity for a *jihad,* a holy war. We never baptize a war. Even when war is necessary, it is still a tragedy.

Here is my fourth truth: *On rare occasions, the alternatives to war are worse than war.*

This truth is expressed in *The Book of Discipline:* "We acknowledge that most Christians regretfully realize that, when peaceful alternatives have failed, the force of arms may be preferable to unchecked aggression, tyranny, or genocide."[3]

Dr. William Sloane Coffin declared last week that "war is a cowardly escape from the possibility of peace."[4] Not always. Don't try to tell that to the brave men and women who helped defeat Hitler in World War II. Surely no reasonable person believes the world would have been better if Hitler had not been defeated.

Many historians believe that if the British and French had intervened in 1936 when Hitler illegally occupied the Rhineland, World War II could have been prevented. The League of Nations was unwilling to enforce its own mandate and the League died.

In 1991 Europeans attempted to solve the problems in Yugoslavia without American help. But when the situation in Kosovo degenerated into genocide, no other nation was willing to act without American leadership. The U.S.-led coalition stopped the genocide and brought war criminals to justice. No responsible leader has suggested that our intervention in Yugoslavia was a mistake.

The prophets of the Old Testament were not always anti-war. Sometimes they urged kings to go to war. Their question was this: "Is war your idea or is it approved by God?"

The great German Lutheran Dietrich Bonhoeffer was a pacifist at the beginning of World War II. Yet before the war ended, he had become part of a failed plot to assassinate Adolph Hitler. The Gestapo imprisoned him. He died at age thirty-nine on a Nazi gallows, stripped of clothes and dignity. His close friend and biographer, Eberhard Bethge, said this about Bonhoeffer's decision to try to kill Hitler: "A Christian should not kill . . . But there are times when you are responsible for human beings around you, and you have to think about all means to stop that man who is killing."[5]

Church tradition assists us in making decisions about war. St. Augustine's guidelines for a just war are still helpful. They are:

First, a legitimate authority must declare the war. In other words, wars must not start because of a personal grudge or an accident. A sovereign head of state must make the decision.

Second, the war must be carried out with a right intention. The purpose must be to protect or restore peace, not to seize land or oil.

Third, the war can be approved only as a last resort. Other alternatives must be tried first. Some say that at this time not all the other alternatives have been exhausted in the Iraq situation. Others disagree, saying that twelve years and seventeen United Nations resolutions are long enough.

Fourth, the war must be waged on the basis of the principle of proportionality. The good to be accomplished by the war must outweigh the suffering and killing that will be unleashed by the war.

Fifth, the war must have a reasonable chance of success.

Sixth, the war must be waged with all the moderation possible. That is, the accepted rules of the Hague and Geneva Conventions must be followed. To the greatest extent possible, civilians and prisoners of war must be protected.[6]

St. Augustine's guidelines are helpful. In addition, there are some special considerations in this conflict with Iraq.

United Nations Resolution 1441 does not only demand the right for inspectors to search for weapons of mass destruction. It demands that Iraq disarm and prove it has disarmed. Where are the twenty-five thousand liters of anthrax the Iraqis had before 1998? Where are the thirty thousand Iraqi munitions capable of delivering chemical or biological weapons? The inspectors have thus far accounted for only seventeen. Iraq has not produced any.

How long can the international community wait? What is a sensible midpoint between a rush to war, on one hand, and an irresponsible flirtation with disaster on the other? Do we really believe that Saddam is using these days of February to comply with United Nations guidelines, or is he rushing toward the deployment of a terrible weapon? Jesus urged us to be "as shrewd as snakes and as innocent as doves" (Matthew 10:16). Is President Bush correct when he says that "trusting in the sanity and restraint of Saddam Hussein is not an option"?

If the United States, Britain and the other allies were to bring their troops home tomorrow and trust that economic sanctions alone will cause Saddam Hussein to behave, would that promote peace or simply convince him and other dictators that they can defy the United Nations with impunity? President Bush and other national leaders must answer these questions. We must pray for them continually.

In the classic movie, *High Noon*, Gary Cooper is the sheriff of a small western town. Earlier a gang of four outlaw brothers had terrorized the town. The sheriff had brought them to justice and sent them to prison. In prison they vowed that when they got out they would kill the sheriff.

The movie focuses on one particular day. The sheriff has just married the beautiful Grace Kelly. She plays the role of a devout Quaker utterly opposed to all violence. The sheriff resigns from law enforcement and the couple is about to leave town on their honeymoon. He plans to start a new life as a rancher. Suddenly word comes that the outlaw brothers have been released from prison and are due to arrive that very day on the noon train. Everybody urges the couple to get out of town quickly.

They ride away, but the sheriff is troubled. Finally he turns the wagon around and heads back to town, much to the consternation of his bride. He cannot stand to run away from his old enemies. He pins the badge back on his shirt.

Quickly, he tries to round up a posse. It is Sunday morning and many folks are at church. The sheriff interrupts the service, explains the emergency, and asks the men of the congregation to help him form a posse. Several people stand up and respond. One of them says, "We'd like to help you, Sheriff, but we're not trained gunmen. That's what we hire sheriffs for." Then another says, "You know, Sheriff, we Christians don't believe in violence." Still another says, "Sheriff, you're a brave man, but it would probably have been wiser if you had not come back to town." The sheriff turns and walks out in disgust. In the background Frankie Lane sings that unforgettable theme song, "I do not know what fate awaits me;/I only know I must be brave,/And I must face the man who hates me,/Or lie a coward, a craven coward,/Or lie a coward in my grave."

How does the movie relate to the crisis with Iraq? Nations are so interconnected now that the world could be compared to a small western town. The United Nations through countless resolutions has declared Saddam Hussein to be an outlaw. The job of sheriff has been thrust on President Bush. We are like those citizens in church. We must prayerfully decide how big a threat the outlaw is, and what we should do about it. May God grant us wisdom and courage. God bless America, and may freedom and justice be his gifts to the entire world.

ENDNOTES

[1] *The Book of Discipline of the United Methodist Church,* 2000, p. 121.

[2] Ibid., 119.

[3] Ibid.

[4] Quoted in *The Commercial Appeal,* Memphis, January 27, 2003, sec. B, p. 1.

[5] From an article in *The Washington Post* by Bill Broadway, reprinted in *The Commercial Appeal,* Memphis, February 1, 2003, sec. F, p. 2.

[6] Quoted in Robert McAfee Brown's book, *Making Peace in the Global Village,* (Philadelphia: Westminster Press, 1981), 42–43.

QUESTIONS

1. Do you agree with the author's assertion that Jesus was not a pacifist? Cite supporting evidence from the Bible.
2. What is the difference between the way the Bible commands individuals to behave in regards to violence and the way nations or leaders are instructed to act?
3. Should Christians ever be eager for war? What is the difference between welcoming war and being prepared for it?
4. Do you agree with the author's position that there is no such thing as a Christian "holy war"? Why or why not?
5. Cite examples from history when a war was the best alternative (in other words, the result of *not* going to war would have been worse than the war itself).

6. Did Dietrich Bonhoeffer and other Christians do the right thing when they attempted to assassinate Hitler during World War II? Why did they fail?
7. Were St. Augustine's guidelines for a just war met before the United States began the war in Iraq?
8. The author wrote this book during the conflict in Iraq, but you are reading it at a later point in history. What lessons can we Christians learn from the U.S. experience in Iraq?

I Have a Friend Who . . .

THINKS HE MARRIED THE WRONG PERSON

EPHESIANS 5:18–21

I have a friend who thinks he married the wrong person. I'm going to refer to this couple as Jack and Jill. They have been married six years. Six years ago Jack was convinced that Jill was the woman of his dreams. She was very attractive, witty, and intelligent. Unfortunately, over the last year or two, the relationship has cooled. He began to notice that Jill was not always attractive. Sometimes, say before nine in the morning, she could be downright unattractive. Jack never mentioned whether or not he himself glanced into a mirror early in the morning. Yes, Jill was intelligent, but there were gaps in her knowledge, rather large gaps. This displeased Jack. He feared that there would be a time when she would embarrass him by making some ill-considered statement in public. Jill had been such a wonderful lover at first. But ever since the baby came along, she seemed to be mostly tired and uninspired. Slowly but surely, he found himself growing cool toward Jill. Now he sees marriage as cornflakes for breakfast and someone sleeping beside you with cream on her face and a retainer in her mouth; marriage is disagreements over finances, visits from her Oklahoma relatives and that grotesque lamp that she selected for the living room.[1] Ironically, though Jack doesn't know it, Jill is having the same doubts about whether or not she married "Mr. Right."

The truth is that every couple goes through some of Jack's and Jill's experience. The romance should not die, but that knee-wobbling, tongue-tied, cross-eyed, heart-pounding, palm-sweating passion phase will pass. The honeymoon phase has to end; otherwise, we could never get anything done. I mean, you wouldn't have missed it for the world, but if that stage were to last, it would wear you out.

Precisely at this point, as the honeymoon phase ends, is a time of maximum danger for a marriage. Satan, our relentless enemy, tries to sell us a big lie. Perhaps he will whisper into your ear, "Hey, girl, just face it. You married the wrong guy. You can't make a silk purse out of a sow's ear. Better just distance from the guy. Go ahead and see a lawyer to help you develop an exit strategy."

Or sometimes Satan's pitch will sound like this: "Hey, big guy, your marriage has lost its zing; that's obvious. Perhaps you picked the wrong girl. Hey, I'll tell you how to be sure. You know the cute little blonde in accounting? She obviously likes you. Start a relationship with her on the side. If you experience a renewed zing with her, then it will be apparent that you made a mistake in your marriage. You're still mighty young. Don't ruin your whole life by sticking with the wrong girl."

What is Satan's real agenda? To separate you from God, to wreck your life and to steal your soul. He wants to wreck your marriage, leaving emotional scars on you and your children so that the next generation will suffer too. Then he wants you to blame all your mess on God so that you will distance yourself from God and miss the cure that only he can provide.

The end of the honeymoon phase is a dangerous time for a marriage, but also a time of great opportunity. The marriage is growing up. With God's help and your best efforts, you can make the marriage better than ever. You can take it to a higher plane. The question is, do you have the faith, courage and commitment to do it?

Ephesians 5:18 commands, "Do not get drunk on wine, which leads to debauchery. Instead, be filled with the Spirit." Paul warns against being under the influence of "spirits," another term for alcoholic beverages, which, when taken to excess, give one a false sense of confidence and well being. Instead, he says, be under the influence of the *Holy* Spirit, who is God's gift to each person who trusts in Jesus Christ as Savior and Lord. It is the Spirit living within you who provides resources for abundant living. But being filled with the Spirit is not a one-time experience. The Greek verb for "be filled" is in the present tense, indicating that the infilling is a continuous experience. Each day I ask for a full activation of the Holy Spirit for the next twenty-four hours. If we don't ask, then the Lord concludes that we think we don't need the guidance and power that the Holy Spirit alone can deliver.

Once we trust in Jesus Christ as Lord and Savior, and the Holy Spirit within us is fully activated daily, certain things naturally follow. Notice verses nineteen through twenty-one. When filled with the Holy Spirit, our conversation is seasoned with grace. We praise God in an authentic way. Worship comes alive.

A church member said to me recently, "In our worship services, I wish we could get the preliminaries over quickly so we can listen to the sermon." I replied, "My friend, those so-called preliminaries are the most important thing we human beings can do, which is to praise God." The Bible says, "God inhabits the praise of his people" (Psalm 22:3; based on the KJV). Pauline Hord, the foremost prayer warrior in our church, reminds me often that "Satan has no power whatsoever over a praising Christian."[2]

In Ephesians 5:21 we discover another result of the infilling Holy Spirit, and this one relates directly to marriage. We are enabled to "submit to one another out of reverence for Christ." I doubt that any couple can genuinely submit to each other over the long haul without God's help. Let's consider how God trains us to submit to each other.

In a Christ-centered, Spirit-filled marriage, the Lord does three things. First, *the Lord corrects.* All of us come into this world with varying degrees of brokenness. That's part of the sad legacy of original sin. All of us have our maladjustments. When we reverence Christ and are filled with the Holy Spirit, we give him permission to mend our brokenness with the glue of his grace. It's an ongoing process that lasts for a lifetime.

An unhappy wife said to a sympathetic neighbor, "My husband doesn't show any interest in what I do. All he cares about is . . . whatever it is that he does at that place . . . wherever it is . . . that he works!"

Christ teaches us to listen, to be more flexible, to be more understanding, to be less demanding, to say the right thing at the right time and at key moments to be quiet.

The poet Ogden Nash said, "If you want your marriage to sizzle with love, / whenever you're wrong, admit it. / Whenever you're right, shut up."

Something else the Lord does for Christ-centered, Spirit-filled couples is this: *The Lord protects.* I do not mean that the Lord shields us from accidents or illness. God does not play favorites in that regard. I mean that he sharpens our consciences so that alarms sound when dangers threaten the marriage.

Remember the classic biblical story of King David who committed adultery with the beautiful Bathsheba. One sultry evening he strolled out on his rooftop to catch an evening breeze. He glanced to an adjacent rooftop and saw a beautiful woman taking a bath. The steps toward adultery were the same then as now. Step 1 was an innocent attraction. David should have looked away. But a little voice said, "Take a good, long look; that is an extraordinary beauty."

Step 2 was curiosity. He wondered if she looked as good up close as she did at a distance, wondered whether her face could match her body. So he sent for her.

Step 3 was high-pressured temptation. Bathsheba was not only beautiful; she was available. Her husband was off with the army fighting a war. David was king, and she was one of his subjects. Can't the King have anything he wants?

Step 4 was lust. The Greek word is *porniya,* the word from which we get "pornography." David gave the "go" signal to lust.

Step 5 was the act of adultery, which later led to the murder of Bathsheba's husband.

If anybody thinks he is above sexual temptation, then he is stronger than Samson, wiser than King Solomon, and godlier than King David. None of us is immune to temptation. But when we reverence Christ and are Spirit-filled, we have some alarm systems that sound warnings.

For example, ladies, let's suppose that a certain man at your workplace often asks your opinion and treats you with courtesy. You think, "Wow! He treats me as really special, which is very different from my husband's attitude." Then the alarm sounds.

For example, guys, let's suppose that at the office there is an attractive woman who is your colleague. You really do have some company business to transact with her. Why not do it over dinner in a relaxed setting? Surely, both spouses would understand. But then the alarm sounds.

When we reverence Jesus and are Spirit-filled, Satan has difficulty casting a spell of *porniya* over us.

Something else happens to married people who are Christ-centered and Spirit-filled: *The Lord motivates.* He makes us willing and even eager to be submissive to each other. This does not mean that we become doormats. This does not mean that we should tolerate abuse. If your spouse ever strikes you or curses you, you are not obligated to remain in that house.

The most confident man in America, Bill O'Reilly, offers this advice: "Don't get married unless you can put your spouse's needs above your own."[3] Good thought, Bill, but I doubt that we can do that consistently over the long haul unless the Lord helps us.

I offer two practical suggestions for couples who are Christ-centered and Spirit-filled.

First, here is a Sunday afternoon challenge. Turn off the TV and skip your Sunday afternoon nap or golf. Instead, sit down with notebooks and pencils, with phones turned off and no distractions. Each of you should answer this question in writing: "What do I like best about the way you treat me?" When you finish, exchange notebooks. Read and talk about what the two of you have written.

The next question to answer in writing is this: "How do you want me to treat you differently?" Again, when you finish, exchange notebooks and talk.

The final question is this: "What do you need from me?"

The second practical suggestion is the "15-5 Plan." Find fifteen minutes each evening, when the TV is off, to ask each other a simple question: "How was your day today?" Each person has seven and one-half minutes to answer, but you don't have to clock it. When you're out of town, do it by phone.

Then before you go to bed, take five minutes to pray for each other. Each of you has two and one-half minutes. Any couple that will use the 15-5 Plan consistently can almost divorce-proof their marriage.

In those marriages in which Jesus does not come first, couples often drift right off the edge into marital failure. But Christ-centered, Spirit-filled couples usually hear a still, small voice within them, saying, "Don't let the dream slip through your fingers. I have called you to a beautiful experience together. Don't bail out before discovering it." Remember, a marriage may be made in heaven, but the maintenance must be done here on earth.

A lady from Ohio wrote to Ann Landers with the following wise perspective on marriage: "Love and marriage are a cycle," she wrote. "The more you do for a man, the more he loves you. The more he loves you, the more he tries to do for you. The more he tries to do for you, the more you love him. And so it goes, round and round. It's so simple. Why don't more people figure it out?"

The reason, dear lady from Ohio, is that many are blinded by sin and selfishness. Some allow the devil to sell them a tragic lie, that they must have married the wrong persons. But happy marriage is much more a matter of *being* the right person than *finding* the right person. If a couple is Christ-centered and Spirit-filled, God can renew and re-infuse their love. Then they will be able, willing and even eager to "submit to one another out of reverence for Christ."

ENDNOTES

[1] William H. Willimon, *What's Right with the Church,* (San Francisco: Harper & Row, 1985), 1–2.

[2] Frances J. Roberts, *Come Away My Beloved,* (Ojai, Calif.: Kings's Farspan, 1970), 127.

[3] Bill O'Reilly, *The O'Reilly Factor,* (New York: Broadway, 2000), 113.

QUESTIONS

1. Why does the author say "the honeymoon phase has to end" in every marriage?
2. In addition to the end of the honeymoon phase, can you identify other times when a marriage is vulnerable to Satan's destructive lies?
3. How can married people, as the author suggests, take their marriages to a "higher plane" during times of testing?
4. After describing how marriages can be severely tested, the author launches into a description of what it means to be filled with the Holy Spirit. What does this have to do with marriage?
5. The Bible tells married people to "submit" to one another. On the surface, this sounds very negative. Is the idea of submitting to each other demeaning to married people? Why or why not?
6. Do you agree with the author that the Holy Spirit provides an alarm system to help protect a Christian marriage? Give examples of how this might work.
7. Are there any instances in which a Christian should *not* stay in a marriage?
8. Why does the author say he doubts people will be able to put their spouses above themselves without the Lord's help?

I Have a Friend Who . . .

IS DABBLING IN NEW-AGE RELIGION

ROMANS 1:21–25; 2 TIMOTHY 4:1–4

I have a friend who is dabbling in New-Age religion, and I'm worried about him. He has views about God and humanity that don't come from the Bible. Much of his reading material comes from the New-Age section of the local bookstore. He refers to God as the "Universal Spirit" and tells me that through yoga and transcendental meditation I can realize my inner divinity.

The first question to ask is: What is New-Age religion? It is a religion that grew out of the spiritual emptiness that many young people felt back in the 1960s. The New-Age Movement is based on an astrological theory that each star age lasts for two thousand years. It is claimed that around the year 2000 we moved from the Age of Pisces into the Age of Aquarius, symbolized by the rainbow. In the memorable words of the musical *Hair,*

> When the moon is in the seventh house,
> and Jupiter aligns with Mars,
> Then peace will guide the planets,

and love will steer the stars.
This is the dawning of the Age of Aquarius.

New Age is a mixture of Eastern mysticism and occult practices, in a Western package. It is sometimes called "hippie values for a yuppie lifestyle." On the surface, parts of it are harmless and maybe even good. It often comes in the guise of self-improvement programs, a concern for world peace, ecology and spiritual enlightenment. Certain elements of New Age are good, like a stress on good nutrition, the avoidance of drugs, and respect for creation. Yoga itself can be a harmless stretching exercise, but beware if a message is delivered along with the yoga. Sometimes under the sugarcoating there is a dangerous pill.[1] As the apostle Paul warns us, "Satan himself masquerades as an angel of light" (2 Corinthians 11:14).

How can you identify New-Age religion when you run across it?

1. Beware when children are taught to chant slogans such as "I can make it happen" or "I am me and I am enough!"
2. Beware of this statement: "I have no use for organized religion, but I am very spiritual."
3. Beware of people who quote books about spirituality but seldom refer to the Bible.
4. Stay away from astrology, horoscopes, or the use of mediums, channeling, or consulting the dead. Such activities are expressly forbidden in Deuteronomy 18.
5. Beware of statements like this: "Good and bad are just relative terms"; "If it feels good, do it"; "I'm okay; you're okay."
6. Beware of someone claiming to be a channel who can put you in contact with someone who has died.

7. Be alert to the fact that New Agers often use the term "Christ-consciousness." It has nothing to do with Jesus of the Bible, but refers only to a spiritually sensitive person.

The influence of the New-Age movement is enormous. One survey found that twenty-five percent of Americans are involved in some form of New-Age practice. Hollywood stars like Shirley MacLaine and Richard Gere are fervent spokesmen for the movement. Some corporations actually employ astrologers.

According to a recent survey, sixty percent of Americans under the age of forty-five reject the notion that one should be limited to a single faith. The result is "an age of mix 'em, match 'em, salad-bar spirituality."[2] New Age is the ultimate salad-bar religion.

It's not hard to see the attraction of New-Age religion. It soothes the ego by pronouncing that the individual is divine. It conveys "spirituality" on someone without requiring any faith or ethical standards. And New Age is optimistic. It teaches that we are progressing toward utopia. We're on an escalator to the stars!

What, then, is wrong with New-Age religion? The short answer is given by St. Paul in 2 Timothy 4:3–4. He predicted that ". . . the time will come when men will not put up with sound doctrine. Instead, to suit their own desires, they will gather around them a great number of teachers to say what their itching ears want to hear. They will turn their ears away from the truth and turn aside to myths."

New Agers reject biblical truth and replace it with their own myths. Here are some particular problems with New-Age beliefs.

First, New-Age religion has a mistaken view of human nature. New Agers say that we are perfect just the way we are. We don't have a sin problem. Our only problem is ignorance.[3] They say that if people would only reconnect with the Universal Spirit, they could realize and express their essential divinity.

But who can say with a straight face, "I am perfect exactly the way I am"? I wonder what New-Age parents think when their child goes through the "terrible two's"? What do they think when their teenager comes home with orange hair, a nose ring, a navel ring and four tattoos? How hard it must be to see the divinity then!

In a scene from Shirley MacLaine's TV miniseries, "Out on a Limb," the star shows how she had to be coached by a New-Age counselor to shout, "I am God," over and over until she could say it with confidence.[4]

St. Paul warned us in Romans 1:23 that either man will worship the true God or he will create a god in his own image and worship it. New Agers fall for that original temptation in the Garden of Eden: "Eat of [this fruit]," the devil said, ". . . and you will be like God" (Genesis 3:5).

The Bible teaches a different view of human nature. Each of us was created in the image of God. However, sin has distorted that image terribly. Outside a relationship with Christ, we are an absolute mess. Christianity is not surprised by the "terrible two's"; our religion anticipates rebellious behavior. Only by repenting of sin and trusting in Jesus Christ as Savior and Lord can the sin damage be brought under control. Only then can we be fundamentally changed. Only through Christ do we have any hope of spending eternity in heaven.

The second problem with New-Age religion is that it distorts the truth about God. New Agers understand God to be an impersonal, abstract force that can be tapped, like an electric current. They refer to God as the Universal Spirit, sort of a spiritual substratum of energy, that is in everything—rocks, people, stars, trees, computers, politics, war and peace, good and evil. In the 1970s feminist leader Gloria Steinem declared, "By the year 2000 we will, I hope, raise our children to believe in human potential, not God . . ."[5] Thank the Lord that Gloria's hope has not come true.

New Agers see Jesus as nothing more than one of the masters like Buddha or Krishna. For them he is not the unique Messiah, Son of God and Savior of the world. In her book, *Going Within,* Shirley MacLaine claims that Jesus was a member of the Essene sect that taught New-Age principles ahead of Jesus' time.[6]

By contrast, we Christians know God to be intensely personal. We can speak to him directly in prayer. He shaped each person in his or her mother's womb. In order to show his love for us, he lived among us as a man named Jesus. He died for us to save us from sin. God has counted the hairs of our heads. He invites us to call him "Abba" or Father.

The third problem with New-Age religion is that it offers no basis for morality. New-Age religion rejects the word *sin* and claims that there are no moral absolutes. If it feels good, do it. Ryan and Travis in *The Wellness Work Book* write, "We will choose to have sex with one another if it enhances our experience of unification with all that is."[7] Because New Agers believe that God is in everything, that means God is in both good and evil; thus there is no real difference between the two.

St. Paul, in Romans 1:24, predicted this kind of false belief. He warned that when people turned away from the truth, ". . . God gave them over in the sinful desires of their hearts to sexual impurity for the degrading of their bodies with one another."

New Agers reject beliefs in judgment and resurrection. Instead, they teach reincarnation, progressively onward and upward. It's an incredible fact that twenty-five percent of Americans believe in reincarnation, and twenty percent claim to have been in touch with the dead.[8] But the Bible declares in Hebrews 9:27, ". . . man is destined to die once, and after that to face judgment."

New Agers fall for another of Satan's lies in Genesis 3:4; he said to Eve, "You will not surely die."

All of this raises an important question: *How should Christians respond to New Agers?*

First, with a double repentance.

If we have dabbled in New-Age beliefs or practices, we should repent and return to the truth of holy Scripture. Maybe we have been drawn into New-Age groups without even knowing it.

One of our church members was part of a neighborhood spiritual growth group. Each member was asked to suggest a book to study. But when she suggested the book of Matthew and it was turned down, she concluded that she was in the wrong group.

Our second repentance should be for our timidity in offering Christ to our friends and neighbors. Thousands of spiritually hungry people are all around us, in our neighborhoods and workplaces. Yet we show little passion for reaching them. We have been like people who have an ample supply of water, but share none of it with their neighbors who are dying of thirst. We should confess to God that we have not been faithful to his final command: ". . . go and make disciples of all nations . . ." (Matthew 28:19).

The second mandate for Christians is this: We should soak ourselves in the truth.

What is truth? Of course the ultimate truth is Jesus Christ. Jesus said, "I am the way and the truth and the life" (John 14:6). Where can we find a reliable account of the truth? In the Holy Bible. All Scripture is "God-breathed" or inspired by God. If God inspired it, you can be sure that it is free of any significant error.

Banks have to be continually vigilant concerning counterfeit money. Counterfeiters are ingenious at producing money similar to the real thing. Most bankers do not train their employees by showing them many different kinds of counterfeit money. Instead they just try to make them thoroughly familiar with genuine currency.

The same principle applies to Christians. *Reading and studying our Bibles faithfully is the best protection against counterfeit versions,* including New Age.

When our younger son Aaron was four or five years old, he was missing several of his front teeth, and of course that affected his pronunciation. Sometimes I would be trying to put together a toy that he had received for birthday or Christmas. Since he knew that I was not strong in the technical or mechanical areas, he would say, "Daddy, read the surrections! Read the surrections!"

That's good advice. Where do we find God's directions for faith and practice? In the Holy Bible.

There is one more thing we should do in response to New-Age religion: *We should offer Christ to New Agers.*

Many New Agers are hungry for truth. They know that materialism won't satisfy. They have this God-shaped hole inside them that is unfilled. New-Age religion won't satisfy because it is not the truth. In a loving, winsome way, invite them to read the gospel of John, one chapter per day, and then talk with you once a week about what they are reading. Invite them to your Sunday school class so they can sample Christian fellowship. Many New Agers are lonely and need a caring community.

Every religion on earth, except Christianity, revolves around the word *do.* Each one offers a list of things one must do in order to reach God or please God or achieve peace. But

Christianity focuses on the word *done*. We celebrate what a loving God has already done for us through Jesus Christ. He visited planet earth. He died on a cross to pay the penalty for our sin. He rose again from the grave and offers abundant and eternal life to all who will simply receive his gracious gift by faith. When your New-Age friend starts talking about his *do* list, share with him the glorious news that all the essential things have already been *done* through Christ.

The big problem with New-Age religion is that it distorts God's Word, and it misses the real Jesus. I love that old gospel song that has this recurring line, "You may have all the rest, just give me Jesus!"

ENDNOTES

[1] Nicky Gumbel, *Searching Issues,* (Colorado Springs: Cook Ministry Resources, 1996), 58. This volume is utilized as a primary resource for this sermon, and references, if not direct quotes, appear at many points.

[2] Kenneth L. Woodward, et al., "A Time to Seek," *Newsweek,* December 17, 1990, 17.

[3] Charles Colson, *How Now Shall We Live?* (Wheaton: Tyndale House, 1999), 268.

[4] Ibid., 269–70

[5] *Saturday Review of Literature,* March, 1973.

[6] Gumbel, op. cit., 67.

[7] Ibid., 63–64.

[8] See "PRRC Emerging Trends," *Atlanta Journal and Constitution,* March 29, 1991, 4.

QUESTIONS

1. Give examples from popular culture and your experience of New-Age attitudes, beliefs and practices. How are they the same as Christianity? How are they different?

2. Why are so many people attracted to the New-Age movement over traditional Christianity?
3. How does the New-Age message tempt us to commit the original sin from the Garden of Eden?
4. Explain the difference between the truth about God revealed in the Bible and the New-Age position that God is an "impersonal, abstract force that can be tapped, like an electric current."
5. The author says the New-Age religion offers no basis for morality. As Christians, why should we live moral lives?
6. The author says Christians need to repent of their own involvement in New-Age practices and also for their lack of passion about reaching others with the Gospel. Can you identify any specific New-Age practices in your life? Do we need to repent of anything else regarding our relationship with the New-Age cults and the people involved in them?
7. How can we protect ourselves from being deceived by counterfeit versions of the truth, such as New-Age thought? List as many actions as you can.

I Have a Friend Who . . .

BELIEVES THAT HELL IS A MYTH

Luke 16:19–31

I have a friend who believes that hell is a myth. He told me that no loving God could consign people to a place of eternal misery. He said that if he were God he would arrange things so that the really awful people like Hitler, Stalin, and Saddam Hussein would end up in an awful place, but for only about twenty-four hours. Then they would get another chance to repent.

Though the subject of hell is frightening, it reminds me of a delightful story. Two American tourists in Italy were taken by their Italian guide to visit Mount Vesuvius, the volcano that still belches forth lava occasionally. They stood on the rim of that volcanic cone and gazed down into a swirling mass of burning, molten lava. One of the Americans said to the other, "That looks like hell." The Italian guide said, "My goodness, you American tourists have been everywhere!"

Many preachers avoid the subject of hell because it is difficult and unpleasant. But the truth about hell is vitally important, and preachers are commissioned to present the whole counsel of God.

The Greek word for hell is *gehenna*. That was the name of a deep ravine south of Jerusalem where in Old Testament times live children were offered as burnt offerings to the pagan god Moloch. That valley was also used as the city dump. It was always smoldering with fire and contained worm-infested carrion. *Gehenna* offered a vivid picture of continuous fire and decay.

Whereas the Old Testament is somewhat quiet about heaven and hell, the New Testament says a good deal. Thirteen percent of Jesus' recorded teachings are about judgment and hell. Hell is mentioned twelve times in the New Testament; Jesus is the speaker on eleven of those occasions. No one spoke of hell more than Jesus did.[1] Jesus said that most people are bound for hell. He taught that we should not be afraid of people who can do nothing more than kill us physically. Instead, said Jesus, we should be afraid of the "One who can destroy both soul and body in hell" (Matthew 10:28; Luke 12:4–5).

No story or statement by Jesus about hell is so graphic as a parable in Luke 16. We know it as the parable of the rich man and Lazarus. Though the rich man has no name, he is often called Dives (pronounced *die veez*), which is the Latin word for *rich*. This finely crafted story is a kind of two-act drama.

Act I takes place here on earth. Dives' only characteristic worth mentioning is his wealth. He wore purple robes costing one hundred dollars in a time when the average daily wage was ten cents. If there had been a Brooks Brothers' store in Jerusalem, Dives would have shopped there. Dives feasted on gourmet food every day and did not alter his daily routine for any religious observances. He was a steak and lobster man. Dives was the epitome of indolent self-indulgence.

Outside the back door of Dives' mansion lay Lazarus, a diseased beggar. It's interesting to note that Lazarus is the only character in any of Jesus' parables who has a name. His name is important. It means literally "one who trusts God." Poor Lazarus was so weak that he couldn't even fend off the dogs of the street that licked his sores. He lived off scraps from Dives' table. In those days there were no napkins. Instead, the rich used large pieces of bread to wipe their mouths and hands and then tossed those scraps on the floor. Those dirty scraps were then swept out the back door by a servant and were consumed by Lazarus and the dogs.

Next comes Act II. Both Dives and Lazarus have died. Death is certainly democratic, coming to Mother Teresa and Adolph Hitler, to Elvis Presley and to an unwanted baby in a refugee camp. Death is the great leveler. Never does anyone get stripped so quickly as he does one second after death.

Suddenly we find Dives in hell and Lazarus in heaven. Lazarus is described in the King James Version as being cradled in the bosom of Abraham. Do you remember the words of this old song, "Rocka my soul in the bosom of Abraham; / O rocka my soul"? I must confess to you that this imagery gives me a bit of trouble. If I'm going to spend eternity cradled on someone's bosom, I think I would not choose Abraham. No offense intended, of course.

We assume that Lazarus went to heaven because he trusted in God. But why did Dives go to hell? Not because he was rich. Abraham was one of the richest men of ancient times, yet he was in heaven. Dives did not mistreat Lazarus. Never did he kick him or order him away from his back door. Why then did Dives go to hell? Because he ignored God and his neighbors. His life was focused on himself.

Using this parable and other scriptural references, our first question is: *What will hell be like?*

Jesus gave us two primary descriptions of hell. First, it is a place of unquenchable or eternal fire. (Mark 9:43; see also Matthew 5:22; Revelation 20:10). Secondly, it is "outer darkness where there will be weeping and gnashing of teeth" (Matthew 8:12; 22:13; 25:30; 2 Peter 2:17; Jude 1:13).

I believe that both descriptions of hell are figurative rather than literal. After all, in Hebrews 12:29 God is called "a consuming fire." But none of us believes that God is some sort of cosmic Bunsen burner. Both the flames and the darkness are symbols of punishment.

Don't think for a moment that I am saying that hell is less miserable than Jesus described. Actually, hell is worse than fire and darkness. The New Testament teaching about hell is meant to appall us and fill us with horror, persuading us that although heaven will be better than we could dream, so hell will be worse than we can imagine. The essence of hell is relational. Hell is total separation from the most beautiful being in the universe—God himself. It is exclusion from anything that matters, from all value, from all beauty.[2]

Hell is punishment, but it's not torture. God is not some sadistic dictator who takes pleasure in seeing people in misery. The thing that makes hell so horrible is the total separation from God. We cannot imagine a place or condition where God is totally absent. About the worst situation we can imagine is a Nazi concentration camp. But horrible as those places were, God was present. Corrie ten Boom and many others testify to his powerful presence there. But hell will be horrible because of God's absolute absence.

Jesus talked a lot about the great separation that will take place at the moment of death. He said, "[The evil people] will go away to eternal punishment; but the righteous to eternal life" (Matthew 25:46). He talked about the separation of the wheat from the weeds, the sheep from the goats, the wise from the foolish bridesmaids. He stressed the urgency of this matter. ". . . Keep watch," he warned, "because you do not know the day or the hour" when the end will come (Matthew 25:13). Never doubt for a moment that Jesus taught there is a hell.

Here is the next great truth related to hell: *God doesn't send people to hell; they go by choice.* In the first place, hell was not designed as a place for people. In Matthew 25:41 Jesus described hell as "eternal fire prepared for the devil and his angels." Hell was not part of God's original creation. It was a necessary add-on as a final place for Satan and his helpers.

God doesn't want any people to go there. Listen to Ezekiel 33:11: "'As surely as I live,' declares the Sovereign Lord, 'I take no pleasure in the death of the wicked, but rather that they turn from their ways and live.'" And in 2 Peter 3:9, we read, "[The Lord] is patient with you, not wanting anyone to perish, but everyone to come to repentance."

In Jesus' story Dives in the agony of hell finally thinks about someone else. He begs father Abraham, "'[Please] send Lazarus to my father's house, for I have five brothers. Let him warn them, so that they will not also come to this place of torment'" (Luke 16:27–28). Whom do those five brothers represent? All of our friends, neighbors, colleagues and relatives who are bound for hell and blissfully unaware of it. They're just as lost as a fire ant on a golf ball, without a clue where they are going. Who will warn them if we do not?

The simple truth is that God sends no one to hell. Those who go to hell send themselves. God gives us a choice and an entire lifetime in which to make that choice. God did all he could to attract us to himself, even to the point of living among us and dying on a cross for us. God did everything except one thing. He did not take away our freedom or force our will. He invites but does not compel. If a person says no to God, that no will be respected for all eternity.

Hell is the end of a path that is chosen here and now, day by day. And only God knows when time is up for each of us. The worst sin one can commit on earth is not child cruelty or wrecking the environment or even genocide. The worst sin is to ignore the all-wise, all-loving Lord of this universe and to disregard the death of his Son for us. That's the ultimate sin. And the only suitable punishment is everlasting separation from God.

As the great British writer C. S. Lewis observed, "There are only two kinds of people in the end: those who say to God, 'Thy will be done,' and those to whom God says, in the end, 'Thy will be done.'"[3] Those persons who end up in hell choose it.

If you don't believe in hell, you declare God to be unjust and the Scriptures to be a lie. Hell is morally justifiable, but it breaks God's heart to see people choose that destination.

Prior to and during World War II, the Nazis told Jews in Europe that if they boarded the trains provided for them, they would be resettled in comfortable, peaceful areas. But the truth was that the trains were headed for Auschwitz and other death camps. Some Jews who knew the truth tried to warn the others, but the majority hushed them up, saying, "That's ridiculous. If you talk like that, you will terrorize people."

Today many church members are being herded aboard another train of false promises called universalism. It is the belief that all persons are bound for heaven whether they wish it or not. Scriptural passages contradicting this false belief are discarded as spurious additions by misguided, judgmental writers.

But real love does not tell people what they want to hear. Real love tells the truth. It does not pretend that a train to Auschwitz is a train to triumph.

There is only one way to be assured of not ending up in hell. That is to repent of sin and to believe that "God loved the world so much that he gave his only Son so that whoever believes in him should not perish but have eternal life" (John 3:16).

Pastor James W. Moore of Houston tells a story about a minister who had a strange dream. He dreamed that he had died and was trying to get into heaven. When he approached the pearly gates, St. Peter told him that he needed one hundred points to be admitted. Proudly the minister said, "Well, I was a pastor for forty-three years."

"Fine," said St. Peter, "That is worth one point."

"One point?" cried the minister. "Is that all?"

"That's it," said St. Peter. "What else can you think of that would commend you?"

"Well," said the pastor, "I visited lots of shut-ins."

"That's worth one point," said St. Peter.

"And I taught the Confirmation Class every year."

"That's worth one point," said St. Peter.

"And I founded a free medical clinic for the poor."

"That's worth one point," said St. Peter. "You have four points now. You need ninety-six more."

"Oh, no," said the pastor. "I feel so helpless, so inadequate. All I can do is throw myself on the grace of God."

St. Peter smiled and said, "Grace of God—that counts for one hundred points. Come on in!"[4]

Every person will spend eternity in heaven or hell. It's easy to by-pass hell. It's just a matter of saying to God sincerely, "I am a sinner for whom Jesus died. I claim him by faith as my Savior and Lord."

If you haven't yet taken that step in faith, do it today.

ENDNOTES

[1] Max Lucado, *When Christ Comes* (Nashville: Word, 1999), 118.

[2] Lee Strobel, *The Case for Faith* (Grand Rapids: Zondervan, 2000), 174.

[3] C. S. Lewis, *The Great Divorce* (New York: Macmillan, 1946), 66–67.

[4] James W. Moore, *Yes, Lord, I Have Sinned But I Have Several Excellent Excuses* (Nashville: Abingdon, 1991), 20 (with some alterations).

QUESTIONS

1. Why do Christians—even preachers—avoid discussing or teaching about hell? Why do so many of us find the subject "difficult and unpleasant"?

2. According to the author, what will make hell so terrible? What do you think will be the worst aspect of hell?

3. What is the best answer to a person who contends, "A loving God wouldn't send people to hell"?

4. Was hell designed for people? If not, for whom was it created, and why? Why do most people think God created hell for evil individuals?

5. If you don't believe in hell, what are you saying about God and the Scriptures?

6. How do you think God feels about hell? Can you give an analogy or metaphor from your human experience that illustrates how God feels when people go to hell?

7. What is universalism? Why does the author call it a "train of false promises"?

8. What is the one way to be sure you do not end up in hell? Why doesn't everyone take this logical step?

I Have a Friend Who . . .

THINKS IT IS WRONG FOR DIVORCED PEOPLE TO REMARRY

MARK 10:2–12; JOHN 4:7–18

I have a friend who thinks it is wrong for divorced people to remarry. Certainly at first reading Jesus' words in Mark 10:11 sound stark and uncompromising: "Anyone who divorces his wife and marries another woman commits adultery against her."

My friend's question gives me an opportunity to shine the light of biblical truth on the huge social problem of divorce in America. If someone reading these words is seriously considering divorce, I hope that he or she will be motivated to try harder to save the marriage. As for divorced people who read these words, I hope you will receive words of genuine grace. We serve a Savior who offers glorious second chances. God concentrates on our hearts, not our histories.

Here are four truths in regard to divorce and remarriage. *First, divorce is always tragic and marred by sin.* The prophet Malachi relays to us this word from God, "I hate divorce" (Malachi 2:16).

An oxymoron is a statement or phrase that contradicts itself. For example, a comfortable Memphis August, or a brief preacher or a fast-paced baseball game. Pastor Bob Russell of Louisville says that "no-fault divorce" is an oxymoron.

Over two million American couples divorce each year. Forty-eight of our states have no-fault divorce laws. Casual divorce is regarded by many as almost a national birthright. One ad in a California newspaper read, "Divorce: $25. Unload that turkey."

But regardless of what the law may say, there is no such thing as "no-fault divorce" in the eyes of God.[1]

In the first century, casual divorce was more common than in modern America. The ancient law of Moses in Deuteronomy 24 prescribed that a man could divorce his wife if he found "some indecency" in her. Note that women had no right to divorce their husbands. No judicial agency governed divorces in those days. All a husband had to do was to write out a divorce decree, and it was a done deal. One rabbi opined that divorce was appropriate if a wife served her husband an unfit meal. Another rabbi approved divorce if a wife spoke disrespectfully about her in-laws. Still another rabbi said it was okay to divorce a brawling woman. Brawling was defined as speaking loudly enough to be heard next door.

Contemporary American culture is like that of the first century in that divorce is a rampant, runaway social disaster. It is the elephant in America's living room, the topic nobody wants to talk about.[2] One generation ago in America, the odds were one in four that a child would witness his parents' breakup. Today the odds are one in two.[3] Family scholar Maggie Gallagher says, "We now live in a society where it is legally easier and less risky to dump a wife than to fire an employee."[4]

Against the lax and permissive background of the first century, Jesus spoke revolutionary words, words that drastically elevated the status of women. Jesus noted that Moses had allowed divorce because of the sinfulness of people, but then he said that divorce was not part of God's original plan. "But at the beginning of creation," Jesus says in Mark 10:6–9, "God 'made them male and female.' 'For this reason a man will leave his father and mother and be united to his wife, and the two will become one flesh.' So they are no longer two, but one. Therefore what God has joined together, let man not separate." Here Jesus declares the ideal of a permanent, life-long marriage. Anytime that ideal is violated, it is sinful.

I have seen divorces in which I thought one spouse was ninety percent guilty and the other spouse only ten percent. But I don't think that any divorced person can claim to be guiltless. There is always a need for confession, even if it is to say, "Lord, I'm sorry that I didn't seek your will more clearly before I entered that marriage."

A divorced woman in our church, whom I will call Jane, shared with me an experience which, with her permission, I share with you. She said, "After my divorce I was angry with God because I felt that my guardian angel had let me down. So I got down on my knees one afternoon and cried my heart out as I asked God, 'Why did you let me down?' Suddenly God seemed to answer, 'Jane, I tried to protect you. I told you not to marry him, but you were stubborn.'" Jane told me that she knew God's answer was right on target. She had known her former husband only two months before they married. Then she added, "People should not get married until they find their soul mate."

We know what divorce does to women. It saps eighty-five percent of their energy just to keep an emotionally even keel going through the day. It cuts their standard of living by two-thirds. It sometimes makes them angry and even violent with their children.

Divorce makes men two times more likely to have heart problems, three times more likely to commit suicide and drastically shortens their life expectancy.

And children are the innocent sufferers. Studies of children tell us that in most cases depression and underachievement will continue for ten years. In fact, one study traced 131 children and found that over half of them still had emotional and psychological problems twenty-five years later.[5] Forty percent of children living with a divorced mother are in poverty.[6]

Divorce is always tragic and marred by sin.

That brings us to a second truth: *Most divorces, but not all, are preventable.*

In this sinful world, some divorces are unavoidable. Some marriages are wrecked beyond repair by mental illness, sexual deviancy and just plain meanness. No spouse should feel bound to remain in a home where abuse is prevalent. Some marriages have deteriorated to the point where it is actually dangerous for one spouse and the children to remain in them. God allows for divorce in such situations. That is why God inspired Moses to write the divorce decree in Deuteronomy. It was a concession to the sinfulness and brokenness of humanity. But even in these tragic cases, divorce for a Christian must be a last resort after every other reasonable remedy has been tried. Most divorces can be avoided, if troubled couples will pray together, worship together and work at communicating.

The devil wants to destroy all marriages. Beware of the lies that he whispers in the ears of unhappy spouses. Lies that sound like this—"Why don't you admit the obvious—this marriage is hopeless?" "You must have married the wrong person." "Why don't you start a little relationship on the side to prove that you can still feel the old zing?" Beware of those lies.

All marriages have stresses and strains. Ruth Graham, wife of Billy Graham, was asked one time if she had ever considered divorce. She replied, "No, but on several occasions I have thought about shooting Billy."

The good news is that those couples who persevere are often rewarded. According to reputable surveys, eighty-six percent of unhappily married people who stay together find that five years later their marriages are happier.[7]

Before filing for divorce, a Christian should ask these four questions:

1. Have I diagnosed the points in the marriage where my sins and failures have caused problems?
2. Have I tried every available resource of professional help? Often men are particularly reluctant to seek the help of a counselor.
3. Has Jesus Christ been given a chance to rule in our home?
4. Is this marriage doing significant and lasting harm to spouses and/or children?

Here is the third truth: *Divorce without repentance leads to tragic remarriages.* Jesus said that any person who divorces his spouse and marries someone else commits two sins: the sin of divorce and the sin of adultery. Yet, back in Deuteronomy, we have God's inspired word telling us that divorce is permissible. This sounds like a contradiction. It isn't. As we have said earlier, divorce always involves sin. If that sin is not faced and confessed, it still stands. That person is still married in God's sight, whatever his divorce decree may say. If that person remarries, the failure rate of those second marriages is terrible. Often the sins of the first marriage are repeated in the second.

Notice that the Bible says, "What God has joined together, let man not separate" (Mark 10:9). Man cannot separate a couple, but God can. Since God established marriage, he alone has the right to dissolve it. The decree of a judge or divorce court is important, but is not enough to cancel a marriage. One is not released from marriage until one has repented and received God's forgiveness and release.

That brings me to the final truth: *We serve the God of second chances.* In John 4, we read about Jesus' encounter with a Samaritan woman at a well. In their conversation the fact came to light that she had been married five times, and at that moment was, as we say, "shacking up" with a guy.

Notice two things. First, this woman was a notorious moral failure. She had been married five times. Nevertheless, that did not prevent Jesus from offering her "the living water" of eternal life. Then note a second fact. Jesus did not instruct her to go find the first man she had married and stick with him no matter how miserable it made both of them (and his current wife). No, our Lord was a realist. He knew that some relationships can be broken beyond repair. He did not condemn such people to wallow in their failures for the rest of their lives. He always offered people new beginnings.

Jesus was and is redemptive. No one is beyond hope. In Christ Jesus there is always a glorious second chance. Divorce is not the unforgivable sin.

Isn't it amazing that the supreme hero of the Old Testament, that man who was the apple of God's eye, was both an adulterer and murderer? And when the prophet Nathan pointed a long bony finger of guilt at David, the king declared in remorse, "Yes, I have sinned against the Lord." And immediately the Lord authorized Nathan to declare, "Yes, but the Lord has forgiven you, and you won't die for this sin" (2 Samuel 12). God forgave and forgot David's sin. What was God's final evaluation of David? He was "a man after my own heart," said the Lord.

Bruce Larson told of a Christian who, before he became a believer, had a habit of using profanity. Soon after becoming a Christian, he got angry and said a profane word. Instantly he fell to his knees and said, "O Father, forgive me for what I said." About ten minutes later, he said another profane word. Again he prayed, "O Father, please forgive me. I did it again." And he heard the voice of God say, "Did what again?"

God doesn't just forgive sin. He remembers it no more. When a Christian genuinely repents of the sin of divorce, and learns the lessons from that failure, God forgives and forgets. Then God is ready to help that believer start anew in marriage if an opportunity comes along.

I conclude with these words by an anonymous divorced person, published in a little pamphlet entitled "New Life."

> Now that the divorce is over, I sometimes think about our wedding day and wonder what happened to that feeling of excitement that swept us along. When did the love begin to fade? Our divorce began long before you moved out of the house. It really began when we stopped communicating thoughts and feelings and needs. It was heralded by long periods of silence and mounting resentments, and finalized by legal maneuvering. Deep down, I knew we were in trouble for a long time, but I just assumed that it would work itself out. It didn't.
>
> What followed was a bit of hell. I felt the whole world was crashing in on me. Nothing had ever hurt so much before. I came through a wasteland of loneliness and a wilderness of pain. But God did not give up on me.
>
> I discovered the most exciting idea known to humankind—that God loves me! At the foot of the cross,

resurrection blooms! Even though I had failed at marriage, even though I had been unloving, even though I had often turned my back on him, God still loves me. God forgives.

With this new awareness, I have learned to love myself and others and God again. New life, new hope, and new peace—these are God's gifts to us. And, like any gifts, all we have to do is reach out and accept them.

ENDNOTES

[1] Quoted from a sermon entitled, "Wisdom for the Divorced," by the Reverend Bob Russell of Southeast Christian Church, Louisville, Kentucky.

[2] William J. Bennett, *The Broken Hearth* (New York: Broadway Books, 2002), 141.

[3] Ibid., 12.

[4] Ibid., 29.

[5] Quoted from a sermon entitled, "Passion for God's Covenant," by the Reverend Greg Lafferty of Christ Community Church, St. Charles, Illinois.

[6] Bennett, op. cit., 149.

[7] Ibid., 158.

QUESTIONS

1. Why is divorce always "tragic and marred by sin"? Can it ever be a positive growing experience for those involved?
2. Why does the devil want to destroy all marriages?
3. List the influences in our society that are tearing marriages apart. What does God want us to do about these problems?
4. Why does the author say everyone who is divorced needs to repent, even if the other spouse is mostly to blame for the split?

5. What does Jesus' attitude toward the Samaritan woman who had been married five times tell us about God's attitude toward people who have been divorced? In light of this, what should our attitude be toward divorced persons or toward ourselves if we have been divorced?
6. After reading this chapter, what is your opinion of remarriage for the Christian who has been divorced? Is this the same view you had before you read this chapter?
7. Despite the risks, are there reasons for Christians to commit to each other through marriage instead of living together as a prelude to marriage? Wouldn't a trial cohabitation prevent "mistakes" in marriage? Cite biblical reasons for your views.

I Have a Friend Who . . .

HAS A PROBLEM WITH WOMEN PREACHERS

ACTS 2:17–18; 1 TIMOTHY 2:11–12

I have a friend who has a problem with women preachers. It's not that he dislikes women. You know, both his mother and wife are women. It's just that he believes St. Paul's guidance to Timothy on this subject was intended to be a universal rule across the centuries. Since he belongs to a church that refuses to ordain women, while we United Methodists gladly ordain women, he and I have had some lively discussions about this matter.

I asked my friend, "Look, if God did not intend for women to teach or preach, why did he make them so verbal?" Stop by any preschool playground and listen to the little people. Little boys make more noises than words. They say "vroom!" and "bam!" and "yea!" But little girls say words, early and often.

I think it was Jean Kerr who said that women speak because they wish to speak, whereas a man speaks only when driven to speech by something outside himself—for instance, when he can't find any clean socks.

Perhaps we should begin this sermon with a word of confession. The church has at times treated women shabbily. Across the centuries the majority of church volunteers have been women, but they have often been discriminated against and underappreciated.

Perhaps you know the story about three people who died and reported to the gates of heaven. The first was a logger from Oregon. St. Peter said to him, "There is a small test you must pass before you can enter. Spell the word *God*."

The logger said, "G-o-d."

"Fine," said St. Peter. "Come on in."

The second person to appear was a rancher from Texas. "There is a test," said St. Peter. "Spell *God*."

The rancher responded "G-o-d" and was welcomed into heaven.

The third person to appear was a businesswoman from New York. St. Peter said, "There is a small test you must take."

"What!" she screamed. "I can't believe it. All my life I had to be overqualified to compete with men. I always had to pass tests that men never had to face. I thought surely when I got to the gates of heaven all of that would be over. I'm so disappointed that you of all people would have a special test for women."

"No," said St. Peter. "This test is not just for women. It's for everybody."

"Oh," she replied, "Well, in that case, give it to me."

St. Peter said, "Spell *Czechoslovakia*."

As I bring the light of holy Scripture to bear on this subject of women preachers, I offer three truths. *First, St. Paul's prohibition against women teachers applied to several local situations; it was not designed as a universal norm.*

Some events and instructions in the New Testament were for the first century only, rather than as normative guidance for all ages. Just because Jesus turned water into wine does not mean that the church should do it on a regular basis.

Remember the setting in the first century. In virtually every culture, women's status was low and opportunities for advancement were practically nonexistent. In Jewish culture, women were not allowed to study. Jews and Gentiles considered it disgraceful for women to discuss issues with men in public. Jews were especially strict, not even allowing women to teach male children past the age of five. Many Jewish men prayed every day, "Thank you, Lord, that you did not make me a Gentile, a slave or a woman."

Then along comes the liberating and revolutionary good news of Christianity, declaring that all persons, regardless of race or sex or class, are equally precious in God's sight. That message knocked those ancient Middle Eastern cultures back on their heels, in much the same way that it is rocking the fundamentalist Muslim cultures today.

For very good reasons Paul cautioned against allowing women to speak in the churches in Corinth and Ephesus. Many New Testament scholars believe that these women, finally relieved of their shackles, were overreacting. Though they lacked the education routinely provided to boys, these women were standing up in church meetings, lecturing the men, putting down their husbands, and threatening the order of the meetings. A taste of freedom can be intoxicating.[1]

Furthermore, some of the women may have been converts from the widespread cult of temple prostitution. They needed to learn, not teach.

St. Paul did not always silence women teachers and preachers. In 1 Corinthians 11:5 we see that women were praying and preaching in the Corinthian Church. St. Paul does not command that they stop, but that they wear a covering over their hair, as women do today when they enter Roman Catholic churches.

In other places Paul allowed women to teach. Priscilla taught Apollos, the great preacher (Acts 18:24–26). In Philippians 4:3, Paul calls a woman coworker "a fellow worker in Jesus Christ."

Paul was reluctant to approve women preachers. But remember, Paul's dominant mission was evangelism. He wanted to reach all people with the gospel. Most first-century men—Jews and Gentiles—would have been scandalized by women usurping authority over men. Therefore, Paul advised a low-profile for women in the church as a local strategy, not as a timeless principle.

Here is the second truth: *St. Paul and the Christian Gospel liberated women to full equality.*

Paul's definitive statement on this matter is given in Galatians 3:28: "There is neither Jew nor Greek, slave nor free, male nor female, for you are all one in Christ Jesus." This was a fulfillment of prophecy from Joel five centuries earlier. Joel declared: "I will pour out my Spirit on all people [says the Lord]. Your sons and daughters will prophesy . . ." (Joel 2:28).

To prophesy really means to preach. The word means *forthtelling* rather than *foretelling*. It means to declare, "Thus saith the Lord," proclaiming the gospel in a compelling way.

A great shift in religious history took place through the life, death and resurrection of Jesus Christ. Women moved, with God's blessing, from a passive to an active role in the church. Women played vital roles in Jesus' ministry, providing hospitality and financial support. They knelt at the foot of the cross on crucifixion day. On Easter morning women were the first persons to see the risen Christ. An angel instructed them to go and tell. If that isn't preaching, I don't know what it is.[2] In

Christ, the perception that Gentiles and women were inferior was abolished.[3]

Here is the third: *Whatever spiritual gift a woman has received, let her use it.*

When St. Paul wrote about spiritual gifts in 1 Corinthians 12 and Ephesians 4, none of those gifts was made gender specific.

There is a rich record of women preachers throughout the Bible. Deborah (Judges 4–5) was anointed as a prophetess, and Isaiah was married to a prophetess (Isaiah 8:3). In the New Testament the prophetess Anna was in the temple when Joseph and Mary presented the infant Jesus (Luke 2:36–38). Also the four daughters of Philip the evangelist were prophetesses (Acts 21:8–9).[4]

Any good Methodist will ask what John Wesley thought about women in ministry. A woman named Sarah Crosby began meeting with a group of Methodists in 1761. They yearned for a word from the Lord, and she felt called to deliver it. Her congregation grew rapidly; from 30 to over 200. She wrote to Mr. Wesley, asking his advice. He responded, "I think you have not gone too far. You could not have done less."

Remember, this was in eighteenth-century England, which was conservative about the proper place of women. There was much opposition to women preachers. One staunch churchman wrote to Wesley, saying, "Sir, a woman preaching is like a dog walking on its hind legs. It is not well done, but you are surprised to find it done at all."[5]

Wesley supported the women preachers but with a bit of subterfuge. He wrote to Sarah Crosby advising her of ways to disguise the fact that she was preaching. One Methodist historian named at least six "women who preached" in early Methodism. Wesley sent this message to a Methodist conference concerning one particular woman preacher: "We give the right hand of fellowship to Sarah Mallet and have no objection to her being a preacher in our connection, as long as she preaches Methodist doctrines. . . ."[6] Whereas it is true that Methodism did not begin ordaining women until the twentieth century, John Wesley's prophetic leadership much earlier charted the course.[7]

Some of my friends in another denomination try to make a distinction between women teaching and preaching. They say it's okay for women to teach Sunday school but keep them out of the pulpit. But that doesn't square with Scripture. In 1 Timothy 2, Paul prohibits women from teaching men, not preaching. In fact Paul urges women to be silent in church. My contention, as I have said, is that that prohibition was for a specific time and place, not designed to be a universal norm.

How much weaker the Christian church would be without the ministries of women like Katheryn Kuhlman, the American preacher and teacher; Mother Teresa; Corrie ten Boom; and Billy Graham's daughter, Ann Graham Lotz.[8]

Women have been the backbone of organized religion in America. According to many surveys by the Gallup organization, women are more religious than men, hold their beliefs more firmly, practice their faith more consistently and work more vigorously for the church. If it were not for women, the Sunday school would fall on its face.[9] Thank God for women in ministry!

Recently, I saw a bumper sticker on a Chevy pickup that said, "The rooster crows but the hen delivers."

One of our church members was in India about four years ago and witnessed an incredible worship service. The evangelist K. A. Paul was speaking to a group of about four hundred women inside a tent. The weather was hot, and the temperature inside the tent was higher. These women were from the lower-class untouchables. Some were Hindu and others had no religious beliefs. Their culture teaches them in a thousand ways that they are worthless. Untouchable women have the highest suicide rate in the world. They can be divorced for any reason and then can do nothing but beg or prostitute themselves.

K. A. Paul stood on a platform in the midst of them and said, "Let me tell you about the God I represent and what he thinks of you." He then invited a little girl to come stand on the platform with him. He asked the crowd, "What is this little girl worth?" He said, "The sari she is wearing is worth about twenty-five rupees, about a dollar and fifty cents. Then her sandals, they are worth maybe 15 rupees, or seventy-five cents. And although I know you would not sell this little girl as a slave, if you did, what would she bring?" In that culture, little girls are often sold into slavery. Mr. Paul said, "She would bring maybe one hundred rupees or five to seven dollars, right?" And they nodded their heads.

Then K. A. Paul said, "The God of heaven and earth has hung a different price tag on this little girl and on every single one of you. In this Bible God Almighty declares that she and each of you are priceless. In fact, God Almighty had only one Son. His name was Jesus. He died on a cross for all of you, and he would have done it for even one of you, even this little girl. He did that to show you how much he loves you, how much he thinks you are worth. If you will trust in him, he will adopt you as his own daughter. Then you will spend all eternity in his presence. Will you accept that offer?"

My friend who witnessed that service told me that he stood there in tears as hundreds of those women streamed forward to say yes to this God who had valued them as priceless.

Aren't you glad to be part of a church that says to all persons, men and women, boys and girls, "You are priceless! Come to Christ, and in Him be all you can be, to the glory of God"?

ENDNOTES

[1] Tony Campolo, *20 Hot Potatoes Christians Are Afraid to Touch* (Dallas: Word, 1988), 37.

[2] George Gallup, Jr., *The Search for America's Faith* (Nashville: Parthenon, 1980), 111.

[3] Campolo, op. cit., 39–40.

[4] Cindy Jacobs, "Women and the Prophetic Ministry," *Current Thoughts and Trends* (August 2003), 7.

[5] Samuel Johnson, quoted in James Boswell's *The Life of Samuel Johnson,* ed. John Canning (London: Methwin, 1991), 91.

[6] Leslie White, *More About the Early Methodist People* (London: Epworth Press, 1949), 170.

[7] Ronald H. Stone, *John Wesley's Life and Ethics* (Nashville: Abingdon, 2001), 162–163.

[8] Campolo, op. cit., 40.

[9] Gallup, op. cit., 112.

QUESTIONS

1. Do you agree that most women are more verbal than most men? Does this give us any insight, as the author suggests, into whether God intended for women to preach?
2. Name specific ways women have been discriminated against and mistreated by the church through history. Does any of this maltreatment continue today?
3. Do you agree with the author's conclusion that the biblical prohibition against women teaching was for the first century only, not a universal norm that still applies?
4. Name some women who are sharing their gifts of preaching with the church today. Have you heard any of

them preach or read any of their books? Do you believe God is using them in the Body of Christ?

5. List all the women in leadership or teaching roles in your local church. If your church is like most, more women than men are involved in its ministry. Is this because God wants more women than men to be involved, or is it because more women than men have said "Yes!" to God's call on their lives? Give reasons for your answer.
6. Have you been part of a congregation that was served by a female pastor? If so, how did the congregation's acceptance or nonacceptance of her affect her ministry?

I Have a Friend Who . . .

THINKS THAT CHRISTIANS SHOULD BE PRO-ISRAEL

GENESIS 17:1–8, 21:8–21; GALATIANS 3:26–29

I have a friend who thinks that Christians should be pro-Israel. I agree with her, but I believe we must also demand justice for the Palestinians. God loves both of these peoples. Both honor Abraham as their forefather, and the Bible includes sacred promises to both. Our mandate as Christians is to work for justice in the Middle East and to share the gospel of Jesus Christ with all who will listen.

Back in 1947 the United Nations sought to divide Palestine into two nations, one for the Jews and one for the Palestinians. The Jews accepted the offer and declared independence. The Palestinians and their Arab allies rejected the UN's offer. There have been recurring wars ever since, always won by Israel. The additional land areas conquered by Israel include the West Bank and Gaza Strip. These areas are bitterly contested today.[1]

Today Israel is a nation of six and a half million people residing in an area smaller than New Hampshire. She is surrounded by twenty-two hostile Arab nations with a combined population of 144 million people. Israel is also opposed by approximately one and a half million Palestinians living in the West Bank and Gaza. In addition hundreds of thousands of Palestinian refugees live in miserable conditions in various Arab countries.[2]

The latest phase in the conflict was triggered by the failure of the Camp David Conference of 2000 when President Clinton, Israel's Prime Minister Ehud Barak and PLO Chairman Yasser Arafat were unable to reach an agreement. Consequently, Arafat launched an *intifada* or uprising. Since then, the Israelis and Palestinians have been at each other's throat.

Their antagonism reminds me of a story Billy Graham tells in his autobiography. He grew up on a farm near Charlotte, North Carolina. His family had a collie dog and there were also lots of cats around the farm. When Billy was a little boy, not knowing any better, he took one of the cats and locked it up inside the doghouse with that collie. They hated each other intensely. But after spending the night inside, they came out the next morning as friends forever.[3] The Jews and the Palestinians are still in the doghouse stage. The morning reconciliation is yet to come.

Let's try to bring the light of Scripture to bear on this complicated situation. Here are three Scriptural truths of great significance in this conflict.

The land of Canaan (or Palestine) was given to all the descendants of Abraham. In Genesis 12:7, the Lord said to Abraham, "To your offspring I will give this land." Again, in Genesis 17:8, we read that "the whole land of Canaan" is given to Abraham's descendants. Abraham's first two sons were Ishmael and Isaac. Ishmael, Abraham's firstborn by Hagar, is considered the forefather of the Arabs. Abraham's second son, Isaac, born of his wife, Sarah, is considered to be the forefather of the Jews. Both of these sons received a covenant promise.

That brings us to a second biblical truth: *God loved both sons of Abraham—Ishmael and Isaac.*

Abraham's love for Isaac was obvious. He was the long-promised son of Sarah, born when Abraham was one hundred years old and Sarah was ninety. Is that a record? If not, it must be close. Those people must have been hardy folks back then. Why did God wait until they were so old to give them a child? So that all generations would know that this was a miraculous pregnancy caused by God.

Reading Genesis 22 will almost break a parent's heart. God orders Abraham to take his son Isaac and offer him as a sacrifice on an altar. Can you imagine anything more difficult for a parent? But then, once God sees that Abraham will obey, God stops him, saying, "Do not lay a hand on the boy" (Genesis 22:12). Abraham (and God) loved Isaac.

God and Abraham loved Ishmael, too. When Sarah demanded that her servant girl Hagar and her son, Ishmael, leave, Abraham was greatly distressed (Genesis 21). Ishmael was his own son. Later when Hagar and Ishmael were on the verge of death in the desert, God sent an angel to rescue them. God "heard the boy crying," and said to his mother, "Lift the boy up and take him by the hand, for I will make him into a great nation" (Genesis 21:18).

Abraham (and his God) loved both Ishmael and Isaac. This is an important biblical truth because it makes it impossible for Christians to reject the descendants of either one.

Here is the third biblical truth: *After the resurrection of Jesus Christ, all Christians are "Abraham's Children."*

The Apostle Paul referred to the church as the "new Israel." In Romans 10:12, Paul wrote, ". . . . there is no difference between Jew and Gentile—the same Lord is Lord of all and richly blesses all who call on him, for, 'Everyone who calls on the name of the Lord will be saved.'"

Paul explains this mystery more clearly in Galatians 3:6–7, 9: "Consider Abraham: 'He believed God, and it was credited to him as righteousness.' Understand, then, that those who believe are children of Abraham . . . . So those who have faith are blessed along with Abraham, the man of faith."

Paul then states this same truth in a negative fashion in Romans 9:8. ". . . not all of Abraham's children are children of God, but only those who believe the promise of salvation which he made to Abraham" (*The Living Bible*).

Paul believed that anyone who trusted in Jesus Christ as Savior and Lord was truly one of Abraham's children, whether that person was born a Jew or a Gentile.

Now, with fear and trembling, let me try to apply these biblical truths to the complicated conflict raging in the Holy Land today. Here are six beliefs that guide my thinking about the Israeli–Palestinian conflict.

First, God's plan for the end of history is not dependent on a particular nation controlling Palestine.

Some Christians interpret certain biblical passages about the end of time to mean that Christ cannot return in final victory until the Holy Land is ruled by Israel and a new temple is built in Jerusalem. I do not read biblical prophecy in that way. God doesn't need our help in ushering in the end-time. He will return in glory when he chooses to, not according to the rise and fall of nations.

My second belief about the Middle East is this: *Israel is the only democracy in the Middle East and therefore deserves the support of the United States.*

Israel is the only country in the region that permits citizens of all faiths to worship freely and openly.[4] Twenty percent of Israel's citizens are not Jewish. By way of contrast, many Arab countries do not permit Jews to live within their borders. Yet in

Israel, Arabs are granted full citizenship and have the right to vote. They are also free to become members of Israel's parliament. Several Arabs have been serving in the Knesset or parliament for a number of years.

The only restriction on Arabs who are Israeli citizens is that they cannot serve in the military. The reason is that they might have to do battle with their own kinsmen.

My point here is that America has a vital interest in Israel's survival.

Here is my third belief: *Suicide bombing of innocent people must always be condemned.* The fact that sixty percent of Palestinians approve of suicide bombers is a real obstacle to peace.[5]

The number of innocent Israeli citizens who have died since the beginning of the *intifada* in 2000, as a percentage of population, would be equivalent to 25,000 Americans dying in the World Trade Center.[6] Wherever terrorism raises its ugly head, whether in Iraq, Afghanistan or Palestine, it must be confronted and defeated.

Hatred of Jews is taught in many Palestinian schools. The peace process cannot advance until Palestinian leaders join in a sustained fight against the terrorists among them, dismantling their infrastructure and changing every school that teaches Palestinian children to hate and kill all Jews.[7]

Here is my fourth belief: *God desires justice for both Israel and the Palestinians.* Remember from the Genesis story that when Hagar and Ishmael were persecuted, God came to their assistance. There will be no lasting peace in the Middle East until the Palestinians have a nation and Israel has secure borders.

The so-called "road map to peace" was drafted jointly by the United States, Russia, the European Union and the Secretariat of the United Nations. It is a significant advance toward justice. Extremists on both sides hate the road map, and that is a good sign that it is fair.

Israel can promote justice by ensuring that no more settlements are built in the West Bank and Gaza. Another significant step would be to stop building or at least redesign the wall or fence that separates many Palestinian farmers from their land and precious water supplies.

On the other hand, the Palestinians can promote justice by stopping Hamas, Islamic Jihad and other terrorists.

Here is a fifth belief: *Freedom is God's gift to all people.* President Bush was right when he declared that "freedom is not America's gift to the world. It is God's gift to humanity." We share with Israel a commitment to "life, liberty, and the pursuit of happiness." And surely we must believe that the same yearning exists in the hearts of most Palestinians. "The human spirit has an unquenchable thirst for freedom, and to gain liberty, human beings will tear down any wall, overthrow any dictator, and escape from any gulag."[8]

The sixth and final belief is this: *Jesus Christ may be the common ground on which Middle Eastern reconciliation can occur.*

Throughout the letters of St. Paul, one feels his yearning for the Jews to be saved. Though Paul was sent as a missionary to the Gentiles, he was himself a Jew and one who loved the Jewish people. In his letter to the Romans, Paul wrote: "Israel has experienced a hardening [of heart] in part until the full number of the Gentiles has come in. And [then] all Israel will be saved" (Romans 11:25–26).

Seventy-five to eighty percent of Jews in Israel regard themselves as essentially secular, as non-practitioners of their faith.[9] On the other side of the conflict, many Palestinians are tired of violence and hungry for the good news of forgiveness and reconciliation. The unconverted human soul does not have the resources to abandon the blame game, to forgive and to achieve genuine reconciliation.[10] Christ can provide those resources. Christ is the only one strong enough to displace all the hate and bitterness. How wonderful it would be if a Christian revival would break out in that beleaguered land! Right now there are only about 150,000 Christians in the entire area of Palestine.[11] But lately the number of evangelical Christians has been growing. Let us pray for a revival there.

I close with a story. In 1913 the Federal government held a fiftieth-anniversary reunion at the great Civil War battlefield of Gettysburg. It lasted three days. Thousands of veterans bivouacked on the old battlefield, swapping stories and reliving those first three days of July 1863. The climax of the gathering was a reenactment of Pickett's Charge. The old Union veterans took their positions on Cemetery Ridge. A half mile away their old adversaries emerged from the woods on Seminary Ridge and started toward them upward across that long hillside. One of the spectators that day wrote, "We could see no rifles and bayonets, but there were many canes and crutches. As the Southerners neared the northern line, the Yankees, unable to restrain themselves any longer, burst from behind the stone wall, and flung themselves upon their former enemies . . . not in mortal combat, but embracing them with brotherhood and affection."[12]

Could that miracle happen between Jews and Palestinians? With men it is impossible, but with God all things are possible (Luke 18:27). There is no hate so hot that the love of Christ cannot cool it. There is no heart so cold that the love of Christ cannot melt it. Let us pray fervently that the gospel of Jesus Christ will be the common ground on which the sons of Abraham discover that they are brothers.

ENDNOTES

[1] Henry H. Halley, *Halley's Bible Handbook* (Grand Rapids: Zondervan, 2000), 1039.

[2] From an April 24, 2002, memo entitled "Twenty Facts About Israel and the Middle East," by Bill Bennett, Jack Kemp and Jeanne Kirkpatrick, under the auspices of Empower America.

[3] Billy Graham, *Just As I Am* (San Francisco: Harper San Francisco/ Zondervan, 1997), 7.

[4] "Twenty Facts . . . ," op. cit.

[5] Larry Derfner, "Road Map to Nowhere," *U.S. News and World Report,* May 12, 2003, 14–18.

[6] Ralph Reed, Jr., in a speech to the Anti-Defamation League, National Leadership Conference, Washington, D.C., April 29, 2003.

[7] Ibid.

[8] Ibid.

[9] An estimate given by Rabbi Micah Greenstein of Memphis, a frequent visitor to Israel.

[10] "Roadblocks and Voting Blocs," *Christianity Today,* August 2003.

[11] Bob Jones, "The War That Never Ends," *World,* May 31, 2003.

[12] Ken Burns, *The Civil War,* (New York: Knopf, 1990), 412.

QUESTIONS

1. Why do you think God loved both Ishmael and Isaac and made a covenant promise with both sons of Abraham, not just with Isaac, who was the son God had promised?
2. Why is it important that we Gentiles are made children of Abraham through faith in Jesus Christ? Does this affect our relationship with Israel in any way?
3. Why should our country be supportive of Israel, the only democracy in the Middle East?

4. What can be done to convince the Palestinian people that suicide bombing, which slaughters innocent people, is not an acceptable method of achieving their goals?
5. Why do human beings desire freedom even more than life itself?
6. Now be honest—what did you think when you first read the author's statement that "Jesus Christ may be the common ground on which Middle Eastern reconciliation can occur"? After considering this, are you going to pray for a Christian revival in the region?
7. Do you think the United States should play a role in resolving the Middle East conflict between Israel and the Palestinians? Why or why not?

I Have a Friend Who . . .

IS DEEPLY CONFLICTED ABOUT ABORTION

PSALM 139:13–16

I have a friend who is deeply conflicted about abortion. She is not alone. So is much of America. In every congregation one can find genuine, compassionate Christians who consider themselves pro-choice and others who see themselves as pro-life. I don't know any Christian who thinks that abortion is a good thing. The distinguished Christian counselor David R. Mace has written, "No sensitive person feels comfortable about [abortion] . . . . But I believe there are situations in which it is justified, as the lesser of two evils."[1]

I recall a beautiful coed who was a member of one of my former churches. She shared with me the fact that she was pregnant because of date rape. I begged her to tell her parents and get their help and advice. But she said that the news would break their hearts so she could not tell them. A friend took her to Atlanta, and she had an abortion.

No one has the right to condemn that young woman unless she has been in the same situation. And even then, it would still be one sinner condemning another sinner, and Christians are warned by our Savior not to do that.

Let's review the facts about abortion. Abortion is the artificially induced premature expulsion of a human fetus, either by surgical or chemical means.[2] Abortion ends a pregnancy by destroying and removing the developing child.

The *Roe v. Wade* decision by the Supreme Court thirty years ago declared that the right to terminate a pregnancy is a matter of personal decision and is a privacy issue protected by the Constitution. Later Supreme Court rulings allowed states to restrict abortion rights in the second and third trimester of pregnancy, but only to protect the health of the mother, not for the purpose of restricting abortions. Since courts tended to interpret "health of the mother" in a very broad sense, abortion has been legal and available even in the ninth month of pregnancy.

No one in 1973 could have guessed how many abortions would be performed in the next thirty years. The peak year was 1990 when 1.4 million abortions occurred in America. Since then the number has been declining, with just over 1.2 million being performed in 1998.[3] Since *Roe v. Wade,* approximately forty million abortions have been performed in the United States. Twenty-six percent of all the pregnancies in America, over one-fourth, end in abortion.[4] About 180 abortions are performed per hour. Here in Tennessee's Shelby County, three abortion clinics together perform approximately five thousand abortions per month, with gross annual receipts of about $2.7 million.

The United Methodist Church declares, "The beginning of life and the ending of life are God-given boundaries . . . Our belief in the sanctity of unborn human life makes us reluctant to approve abortion. . . . We recognize certain tragic conflicts of life with life that may justify abortion, and in such cases we support the legal option of abortion under proper medical procedures."[5]

Most of us recognize that in cases of rape, incest or direct threat to a mother's life, many Christians may consider abortion. But all of those situations account for no more than three percent of the abortions in America. My focus today will be on the other ninety-seven percent, those abortions that are elected either because the baby would create a hardship for someone or because the mother doesn't feel ready for the baby or because someone else wants her to have an abortion.

What does the Bible say about abortion? Actually, the word "abortion" is not in the Bible. However, the leaders of the early church discussed the matter at length, and it was universally condemned.[6] Many Bible passages relate to abortion. One of them is Psalm 139:13–16.

In these verses God inspired King David to marvel about the origins of a human life. Note that he did not begin with the baby's birthday. No, he backed up almost a year earlier. Verse 16 says that God "saw my unformed body," the pre-embryonic substance that was to become my body. God sees a baby even before a sonogram can project its tiny body on a TV screen.

Verse 13 declares that God "knit me together in my mother's womb." There could be no stronger statement concerning the dignity and sanctity of the unborn child than this.[7] You know, we find it almost impossible to do anything creative without at least a little light to work by. Yet God does some of his very best work in the dark of a mother's womb.[8]

Verse 14 declares that each of us is "fearfully and wonderfully made." A baby's hand fascinates me. Check out the tiny fingernails and little wrinkles. The Lord's detail work is amazing.

A cynic could reply, "You can say the same thing about puppies and bear cubs and baby baboons—they are fearfully and wonderfully made." Yes, but verse 13 sets human beings apart. It says, "You created my inmost being." That refers to our human distinctiveness. It's in our heads. No wonder our heads are bigger in relation to our bodies than other creatures. We have the unique capacity to know God, to make moral decisions and to envision eternity. Why are we different? Genesis 1:27 explains that we are made in the image of God. The Bible does not say that we take on the image of God after six months of development within a mother's womb. It says that we existed in the mind of God before the moment of conception. The prophet Jeremiah heard God saying to him, "Before I formed you in the womb I knew you" (Jeremiah 1:5).

Notice in Psalm 139 that God maps out a plan for every new baby. "All the days ordained for me were written in your book before one of them came to be." Oh, I wonder how different America would be if the forty million victims of abortion since 1973 had lived. God's roster has so many missing players. And note this—if ordaining the days of a person's life is God's right, then no one else should do it.[9]

With this Scripture as background, I declare four truths about abortion.

First, an unborn child is sacred and priceless. Why? Because each child is made by God and in the image of God. Even an atheist holding a baby looks helplessly to heaven for somebody to thank.[10]

Do you remember the great gospel singer Ethel Waters? Who could ever forget the way she sang "His Eye Is on the Sparrow" at Billy Graham Crusades? She wrote in her autobiography that she was conceived following the rape of her thirteen-year-old mother. Yet she too would have said, "I praise you, Lord, for I am fearfully and wonderfully made."[11]

Here is the second truth: *America is changing her mind about abortion.* The peak year for abortions was 1990. The number has been declining ever since. An editorial in *USA Today* said, "A quiet shift is occurring, one choice at a time."[12] Among college freshmen, a notoriously liberal lot, approval of abortion has dipped ten percentage points in the past decade. A Zogby Poll released in December 2002 found that thirty-two percent of Americans have changed their minds about abortion in the past decade, with twenty-one percent saying they viewed abortion more negatively, while only eleven percent viewed it more positively.[13]

Part of the reason is that technological advances, like the sonogram, have allowed us to observe life directly as it develops within the womb. We know that by day twenty the foundations of the brain, spinal cord, and nervous system are already established. By day twenty-one the heart begins to beat. Surgical abortions are usually not performed before the forty-ninth day. By that time, the baby has identifiable arms and legs and displays measurable brain waves.[14]

Another reason that abortion rates are declining is because of the suffering that parents have experienced over the last thirty years. A woman from Illinois wrote to *Time* a few years ago and said, "For the set of circumstances I faced at age twenty-four, abortion was the only alternative I could find. I just wish that when I had gone for counseling at the family-planning clinic, I had been told that the momentary pain of the procedure was nothing compared to the ache in my heart for a lifetime."[15]

Harold O. J. Brown expressed the sentiments of many when he said, "Whatever you think of abortion, it cannot be good to kill one-fourth of every new generation."[16]

That points me to a third significant point: *Help is available for women with difficult or unwanted pregnancies.* Many experts believe that most women choose abortion out of a lack of practical resources and emotional support. That kind of support is now more available than ever before. Life Choices is one of the great organizations reaching out to women and/or couples facing a crisis pregnancy.

Here is the fourth and final truth about abortion: *God's grace can heal the wounds that remain after abortion.* Millions of parents have been burned by abortion. Grieving is a normal and healthful response to a major loss through death. It is a painful process that often includes stages of denial, anger and the need to forgive as well as to be forgiven. God still loves you. Abortion is not the unforgivable sin. Nothing you could do would make God love you more, and nothing you have done could make him love you less. God is so eager to lift your burden. If you say to him sincerely, "I'm sorry, Lord, please forgive me," his forgiveness is instantaneous, thanks to the cross. Not only that, he will teach you to forgive yourself. God longs to embrace you and to wipe away your tears. In heaven you will have all eternity to enjoy the little one you never met here on earth.

Dear parents, if your unmarried daughter ever comes to you and says, "I'm pregnant," whatever you may be feeling and however your stomach may be churning, please stay calm and do not assign blame. Focus on the positive. She could have chosen abortion. Show grace and mercy as Jesus would, even when it's toughest. And for goodness sakes, hug her and say, "We love you and we're going to come through this together."

And you men, don't ever tell a woman to have an abortion. Don't ever threaten that if she doesn't, you won't have anything to do with the baby or her. She has enough on her plate without having you add to her burden.

I repeat the truths that I want to plant in your heart regarding abortion: An unborn child is sacred and priceless. America is changing her mind about abortion. Help is available for women with difficult or unwanted pregnancies. Finally, God's grace can heal the wounds that remain after abortion.

Do you remember the furor created some years ago when a man attacked Michelangelo's magnificent *Pieta* in Rome? This glorious and beautiful statue of Mary holding the dying Jesus has been viewed by millions. A deranged man went after it with a hammer. The news of that disaster was beamed around the world.

But the *Pieta,* magnificent as it is, cannot compare to the wonder of an unborn child. He or she is truly a masterpiece. Only God can create a human life with his very image stamped upon it, and only God has the right to determine at what point each human life transitions from this world into eternity.

ENDNOTES

[1] David R. Mace, *Abortion: The Agonizing Decision* (Nashville: Abingdon Press, 1972).

[2] "Abortion—Some Medical Facts," NRL Educational Trust Fund, Washington, D.C., 5.

[3] Adam Hamilton, *Confronting the Controversies* (Nashville: Abingdon Press, 2001), 99.

[4] William J. Bennett, *The Broken Hearth* (New York: Broadway Books, 2001), 18.

[5] *The Book of Discipline of the United Methodist Church*—2000, Nashville: United Methodist Publishing House, 102.

[6] Hamilton, op. cit., 104.

[7] Donald M. Williams, *Psalms 73–150,* Vol. 14 of The Communicator's Commentary, ed. Lloyd J. Ogilvie, (Dallas: Waco Books, 1989), XIV: 485.

[8] Charles H. Spurgeon, *Spurgeon on the Psalms* (Grand Rapids: Kregel Publications, 1968), 639.

[9] Lee Eclov, "Choose Life," *Preaching Today* (Editorial@Preaching Today.com).

[10] Ibid.

[11] Ibid.

[12] "Abortions Decline," *USA Today,* January 11, 2001.

[13] Bob Jones, "30 Years Later," *World,* January 18, 2003, 19.

[14] Hannibal Hamlin, M.D., "Life or Death by EEG," *Journal of the American Medical Association* (October 12, 1964), 113.

[15] Letters to the Editor, *Time,* March 24, 1995.

[16] Harold O. J. Brown, "Religion and Society Report," February 2001, 5. (Reproduced in *Current Thoughts & Trends,* August, 2001, 24).

QUESTIONS

1. Why has the number of abortions performed annually in the United States been declining since 1990?
2. Many Christians consider abortion acceptable in cases of rape, incest or direct threat to a mother's life. What do you think about these "exceptions"?
3. Why is it significant that God inspired David to write in what we now call Psalm 139 about the wonder of the developing baby rather than a newborn baby?
4. Is a fertilized egg made in the image of God? An embryo? A fetus? Can we say when a human being is created in God's image?
5. How can Christians opposed to abortion help put an end to the tragic practice?
6. What should a Christian's attitude be toward to an unmarried woman who becomes pregnant? Toward a women who has had an abortion?
7. Does the media adequately report the misery and grieving experienced by parents who lose a child to abortion?

I Have a Friend Who . . .

LIVES WITH HER BOYFRIEND

1 Corinthians 6:9–20

I have a friend who lives with her boyfriend. When I asked her about this arrangement, which is clearly contrary to biblical standards, she replied, “We are just experimenting to see if we can get along together before we make a final decision about marriage. My boyfriend’s parents went through a divorce that was very hurtful to the whole family, and we certainly want to avoid that.”

My friend’s situation is not uncommon. There are many cohabiting couples, some with high visibility. Recently David Letterman announced on his TV show that he and his girlfriend Regina were going to have a baby. He said, “I realize we kind of got the cart before the horse here. But I’m just seeing how much I can get away with.”

Oprah Winfrey has been modeling this kind of arrangement for a long time. So have movie-star couples like Susan Sarandon and Tim Robbins, Goldie Hawn and Kurt Russell and Jessica Lange and Sam Shepard.

Between 1960 and 2000, the number of cohabiting couples in America increased elevenfold, to five and a half million. Today over half of all marriages are preceded by a period of living together.[1]

A couple named Janna and Stephan, both in their early thirties, fell in love ten years ago while attending college. Today they live together, having made a firm commitment not to make a firm commitment—to marriage, that is. They told *USA Today,* "We didn't want a relationship based on some false sense of security. Our relationship is about getting up each day and treating each other with respect and love. We don't need a marriage license to give us that."[2]

For a biblical perspective on cohabitation, we turn to 1 Corinthians 6:9–20. In verses 9 and 10, Paul lists ten categories of sinners who will not be in the kingdom of God. At the top of his list he indicts the "sexually immoral." The Greek word is *porneia,* a word meaning *fornication,* which is a sexual relationship between an unmarried person and someone of the opposite sex. Paul is not saying that people guilty of these ten sins cannot be saved. But he is saying that those who persist in these evil practices without repentance will not be part of the kingdom of God.

Verse 11 gives us enormous confidence. Paul reminds the Corinthians that they were guilty of those same sins, but they "were washed." That means that by confessing their sin and trusting in the sacrifice of Christ on the cross, their sin was washed away. Remember the words of the old hymn: "What can wash away my sin? Nothing but the blood of Jesus."[3]

Verse 12 points us to a heresy (a false belief) that was popular in ancient Corinth and is alive and well in contemporary America. I am referring to a libertine attitude that says, "Look, since I am covered by the forgiving grace of God, I can do whatever I please. Sin is no big deal."

Paul responds, "That is ridiculous! Though I am a free person in Christ, my behavior is vitally important. It will either glorify or detract from the Lord I serve."

In verse 13 Paul writes, "The body is not meant for sexual immorality, but for the Lord." In verse 16 Paul reminds us of the definitive standard for Christian sexuality. It was first stated in the Genesis account of creation. Later Jesus reaffirmed it when he said, "A man will leave his mother and father and be united to his wife [not his girlfriend] and the two will become one flesh" (Mark 10:7–8).

The Bible in both the Old and New Testaments affirms the lifelong, monogamous union of a man and a woman as God's exclusive norm. The Bible offers no positive examples of non-martial sex; and it specifically condemns fornication, adultery, and homosexuality as forms of sin.[4] The biblical standard for sexuality is simply fidelity in marriage and celibacy in singleness.

In Galatians 5:19 Paul declared, "The acts of the sinful nature are obvious." And then he listed the obvious sins. First on the list is sexual immorality or fornication.

In 1 Corinthians 6:18–20, Paul claims that sexual sin is different and in a sense worse than any other kind of sin. He reminds us that when we became believers we were bought or redeemed by the shed blood of Christ. We were grafted into Christ as one might graft one branch of a tree into another. The Holy Spirit took up residence within us. We became temples of the Holy Spirit.

When we commit sexual sin, we break down the grafting process and drive out the indwelling Christ. Sexual sin is the most intensely personal of all sins. When Jesus gave us a list of sins in Mark 7:21, he put fornication next to the top of the list.

I like the way Eugene Peterson summarizes Paul's message in our text for today. He writes, "There's more to sex than mere skin on skin. Sex is as much spiritual mystery as physical act. In sexual sin we violate the sacredness of our own bodies, these bodies that were designed for 'becoming one' with another person in a lifetime covenant."[5]

This biblical message related to cohabitation raises three questions. First: *Why do unmarried couples decide to live together?*

One of the reasons is the oldest temptation known to man—the possibility of having some of the privileges of marriage without any of the responsibilities. In past years women exerted some pressure in helping men resist that temptation. Remember the words of the old song, "Love and marriage, love and marriage,/Go together like a horse and carriage./Dad was told by mother,/'You can't have one without the other.'"

However, in recent years, with birth control and sexual liberation, many women seem to be as tempted as are some men to a libertine lifestyle. In Christina Aguilera's new Grammy-nominated video called "Dirrty," she has a song entitled, "Get Mine, Get Yours." It includes these words: "We have a physical thing. We'll make love, but don't fall in love."[6]

A second reason for the increase in cohabitation is the influence of modern feminism. Gloria Steinem declared in 1987 that she was unlikely to marry because in wedlock a woman becomes a "semi-non-person." But she later changed her mind. In 2001 Ms. Steinem, at the age of sixty-six, became a first-time bride and declared herself to be "happy and surprised."[8]

Surely the major reason for the increase in cohabitation is the widespread myth that if a couple has a period of living together before they marry, it might prevent bad marriages from occurring, and is excellent marriage preparation for good relationships. In May 2003 the *Commercial Appeal* newspaper of Memphis ran a feature article entitled "Cohabitation Nation." It quoted one of the cohabiting couples as saying, "Living together is a matter of practicality not morality. It's a necessity to live together before you get married."[8] But since when do we decide by popular vote what the moral issues are? That's God's business. If we humans could decide what constitutes a moral issue, before long you would have the mayor of a major city declaring that casino gambling in a local sports arena is not a moral issue! God identifies the moral issues, and sexual activity outside of marriage is on God's list.

That leads to the next question: *What are the facts about cohabitation?*

Virtually all research proves that cohabitation is not good preparation for marriage. In June 2002, social science researchers David Popenoe and Barbara D. Whitehead published their findings after reviewing nearly fifty cohabitation studies that spanned nearly a decade. They concluded that people who live together before marriage are forty-six percent more likely to divorce than those who do not. Only one-sixth of all cohabiting couples are still together after three years. Only one-tenth of them last five years or more. For most people, cohabitation is an inherently unstable arrangement.

Cohabitation increases the risk of domestic abuse against women plus the risk of physical and sexual abuse of children. It also increases the likelihood of both depression and sexual unhappiness. Cohabiting men are four times more likely to be unfaithful to their partners than are married men.[9]

Cohabitation undermines lasting attachments, mutual obligations, successful child rearing and sexual fidelity. What it offers instead is a kind of institutionalized adolescence—a dream of free love without responsibility or commitment.[10]

That brings us to a final question: *What does a Christian marriage have that most cohabitating arrangements lack?*

The answer is three things, each starting with the letter *C*, each one of crucial importance to a happy marriage.

The first is *commitment*. Virtually all research shows that most cohabiting couples are less committed to each other than are married couples. And if these live-ins go on to marry, fifty percent will separate within five years, compared with about twenty percent of married couples.[11] Are some cohabiting couples committed to each other? Of course. But most of them have a real problem saying to each other, in front of God and everybody, "I am committed to you, for better or worse, in sickness and in health, till death us do part." If a man and woman enter a relationship with an exit option, usually one of them will take it.

Part of the mystery and glory of marriage that cohabiters seldom understand is this shared understanding by married couples that whatever the future brings, they are committed to each other for the duration. Such commitment releases people for glorious openness, honesty and trust. And according to most research, it makes for the best sexual relations on earth.

The second *C* word is *cherishing*. A newspaper publisher in Washington, D.C., had a long-running affair with a prominent businesswoman. One day Sally issued Ben an ultimatum—either you marry me or our relationship is through. He asked her, "Why the sudden change? Why this desire for marriage?" She replied, "I have finally realized that whereas men often love their girlfriends, they truly cherish only their wives. And I want to be cherished."

To cherish means to treat as dear, to nurture tenderly and to treasure. It is no accident that the marriage vow includes the promise "to love and to cherish."

The third and most important thing that marriage can have but cohabitation does not is *Christ*. It is impossible to persist in a known sin without forfeiting the intimacy of Christ. He loves us sinners. But when we stubbornly continue in conduct that we know from the Bible to be wrong, we drive him out from his controlling place in our hearts and relationships. This is why St. Paul called sexual immorality worse than other sins. It is such an intensely personal sin that it drives out the Holy Spirit from our hearts, which are designed to be his temples.

When I counsel with couples preparing to marry, and if I know they are already living together, I say something like this: "Dear ones, I know that a great marriage requires the presence of Christ in our hearts and homes. Otherwise selfishness and other sins are too powerful to resist. Yet you two are structuring your relationship now in a way that is contrary to God's revealed will. Therefore, you are telling God that you don't need him. You *do* need him. If Christ is not Lord of your home, you will miss vital help and awesome joy. Would you prayerfully consider changing your living arrangement so that you go into this marriage wide open to all the blessings God can give?"

Professor Leon Kass summed up the matter quite well when he said, "Marriage is not something one tries on for size and then decides whether or not to keep. It is rather something one decides with a promise and then, assisted by the grace of God, bends every effort to keep.[12]

ENDNOTES

[1] William J. Bennett, *The Broken Hearth* (New York: Broadway Books, 2001), 13.

[2] Ibid., 75.

[3] Robert Lowry, "Nothing but the Blood," 1876.

[4] Stephen F. Noll and Todd H. Wetzel, "Biblical Foundations for Morality and Sexuality," *Confessing the Faith,* ed. Craig M. Kibler (Lenoir, N.C.: Reformation Press, 2003), 177.

[5] Eugene H. Peterson, *The Message* (Colorado Springs: Navpress, 2002), 346.

[6] Janice Shaw Crouse, "Get Mine, Get Yours," *Christianity Today,* May 2003, 67.

[7] Bennett, op. cit., 77.

[8] "Cohabitation Nation," *Commercial Appeal,* May 23, 2003.

[9] Neil Warren, "The Cohabitation Epidemic," *Focus on the Family,* June–July 2003, 10–11.

[10] Bennett, op. cit., 77–81.

[11] From a body of research by sociologists Pamela Smock of the University of Michigan and Wendy Manning of Bowling Green State University, quoted by *USA Today*, September 18, 2003, 8A.

[12] Statement by Leon Kass, quoted in *Marriage Partnership,* Fall 1996, 69.

QUESTIONS

1. Why do so many people today live together without being married?
2. Some of the reasons people give for living together without marriage are pretty convincing. Why does God say in the Bible that it is wrong?
3. Give examples of ways our culture rejects the biblical standard of fidelity in marriage and celibacy in singleness.
4. Why is sexual sin so destructive to us as human beings?
5. Some couples feel that living together is a matter of practicality, not morality. What practical benefits of cohabitation might they believe outweigh its disadvantages? What is the danger in considering only practical advantages such as having one rent payment?
6. Why doesn't living together before marriage prevent bad marriages?

7. Why might marriage lead to better and more satisfying sexual relations than cohabitating?
8. Why does a great marriage require the presence of Christ in the participants' hearts and home?

I Have a Friend Who . . .

STRUGGLES WITH HOMOSEXUALITY

JOHN 8:3–11; ROMANS 1:24–27

About a month ago, my friend John stopped me after a worship service. He said, "Brother Bill, I noticed that you are going to be preaching about homosexuality in a few weeks. I want you to know that I have struggled with homosexuality for a long time. Actually that is what broke up my marriage. I have been through lots of pain. Several years ago I began seriously to seek God's help. I set out to find a church. In one church that I visited, the minister referred to homosexuals in an extremely negative, angry way, calling them names that were hurtful to listen to. I certainly did not feel at home there. Then I found another church that was the opposite. The preacher said that the Bible approves all kinds of sexual relationships between consenting adults who care for each other. Well I knew enough of the Bible to know that he was not telling me the truth. I figured that if he would lie to me about one part of the Bible, he would do so about another. So I got out of there. And then I found Christ Church. I could tell right away that you are Bible-centered and would always tell me the truth. But I also sensed that you wouldn't beat me over the head with the truth. I felt kindness and acceptance here, so this is where I have made my home. By the grace of God I have been able to lead a celibate life, and I feel very fulfilled. Thanks for your hospitality."

I must confess that I had tears in my eyes when John finished talking.

His words assured me that we were being faithful to our commission. Our task as a church is to oppose sin but love sinners. We must never pretend that wrong is right. And we must never forget that even the most despicable sinner is just a whisper of faith away from being a redeemed child of God.

During the last twenty years, American culture has been subjected to a major marketing campaign designed to persuade us that homosexuality is a normal and valid lifestyle. The National Gay and Lesbian Journalists Association, made up of writers and editors of the largest media outlets in the nation, including *USA Today, Time, Newsweek* and *The New York Times,* ensures regular and positive presentations of the homosexual agenda. Though practicing homosexuals constitute no more than four percent of our population, they have enormous influence in our culture. The goal of the homosexual activists is social approval and legal endorsement for homosexuality. Their single most important goal is to gain legal recognition for same-sex unions or homosexual marriage.[1] This marketing campaign has been remarkably successful. The Episcopal Church has ordained a practicing homosexual as bishop. Newspapers such as the *Washington Post* and *The New Orleans Times-Picayune* have begun to run "marriage" announcements for homosexual couples. Several months ago New York City officials established the nation's first high school for homosexual students. Many major American companies grant marriage benefits to same-sex partnerships.

So successful has the marketing campaign been for homosexuality that across America a kind of political correctness prevails that regards any criticism of homosexuality as the equivalent of racism.[2]

Singer and actress Barbara Streisand said, "I believe everyone has the right to love and be loved, and nobody on this earth has the right to tell anyone that their love for another human being is morally wrong." Of course, Barbara is not talking about plain love; she is speaking of sexual love.[3] And in regard to sex, the Bible has a very clear standard that we must uphold. That standard is fidelity in marriage between a man and a woman and celibacy in singleness.

The Bible is univocal on the subject of homosexuality. Ten scriptural passages relate to homosexuality. Those ten are: Genesis 1:27; Genesis 19:4–11; Leviticus 18:22; Leviticus 20:13; Judges 19:20–28; Mark 10:8; Romans 1:24–27; 1 Corinthians 6:9; 1 Timothy 1:10; and Jude 1:7.

The Romans 1:24–27 passage is the single most important of those ten. It is the only passage in the New Testament that explains why homosexual activity is wrong. Verse 24 begins with the word *Therefore*. It refers to verse 21. There Paul indicts the wicked for failing to glorify the God they knew. When God is disregarded, usually man worships himself. As Paul tells us in verse 25, idolatry is the sin behind homosexuality. Idolatry is the worship of someone or something other than God. Often when man worships himself and his own pleasure, sex is deified and perverted. The creation is corrupted. Verse 24 tells us that God "gave them over" to sexual impurity. This means that God allowed sin to run its course as an act of judgment. Then in verses 26 and 27

Paul mentions lesbianism and homosexuality as particularly graphic examples of how sin distorts God's created order.

Paul does not equivocate about homosexuality. Dr. Robert A. J. Gagnon, a professor of New Testament who has written the definitive work in this field, declares that same-sex intercourse "is strongly and unequivocally rejected by Scripture because it violates the gendered existence of male and female ordained by God at creation."[4]

The United Methodist stance on homosexuality is in accord with Scripture. *The Book of Discipline* contains the following guidelines: No homosexual unions can be performed in our churches and no church funds can be given to organizations promoting the acceptance of homosexuality. Self-avowed, practicing homosexuals cannot be ordained. At the same time, we United Methodists are committed to support the human rights and civil liberties of all persons. Believing that all persons are of sacred worth, we are committed to minister to and with all persons. Although we do not condone the practice of homosexuality and consider this practice incompatible with Christian teaching, we affirm that God's grace is available to all.

Having expressed the biblical and United Methodist perspectives on this subject, I offer four truths.

First, all sexual activity outside of marriage between a man and a woman is sinful. All ten Scriptures relating to homosexuality are opposed to it.

Some homosexual activists try to convince us that homosexuality is genetically determined, and therefore it must be God's will for those persons. There is no definitive scientific evidence to support such a theory. David Persing, a molecular genetics researcher and a Christian, points to the biblical teaching that all of nature is corrupted by sin. This could include natural tendencies toward various forms of sinful behavior, from alcoholism to heterosexual addiction to homosexuality. Christianity calls all of us to struggle against these natural tendencies rather than to surrender to them.[5]

We should remember that homosexual orientation is not a sin. The Bible does not condemn homosexual feelings or temptations. Temptation is not sin. Jesus was "tempted in every way, just as we are—yet was without sin" (Hebrews 4:15). The Bible condemns homosexual practice, not preference.

Here is the second truth: *Unrepented sin has consequences.* I do not like the term *gay* because it is a misnomer. The traditional meaning of the word is lighthearted, jolly and carefree. But the homosexual lifestyle is usually sad, sickly and sometimes tragic. According to Bob Davies, executive director of Exodus International, twenty-five to thirty-three percent of homosexuals are alcoholics, compared with seven percent of the general population. Homosexual men are six times more likely than straight men to attempt suicide.[6]

Psychiatrist Jeffrey Satinover, in *Homosexuality and the Politics of Truth,* points out that the likelihood of homosexual men contracting HIV is four hundred times the likelihood of heterosexual men contracting it. Homosexual persons compose fewer than five percent of America's population but account for eighty percent of the sexually transmitted diseases.[7]

Lesbians are six times more likely to be substance abusers than are heterosexual women.[8] A survey in 1991 and 1992 found that homosexuals not suffering from AIDS had a life expectancy of forty-two years, compared to over seventy years for the general population.[9] As I said, the homosexual lifestyle is sad, sickly and sometimes tragic.

Here is the third truth: *If we repent of sin, God is eager to forgive and transform.* God loves the person practicing homosexuality just as much as he loves any of the rest of us sinners. God sent

Jesus Christ to die on a cross so that all of us sinners could discover forgiveness and salvation. As the Bible promises, "If we confess our sins, God is faithful and just and will forgive us our sins and cleanse us from all unrighteousness" (1 John 1:9).

God is not the Great Rubber Stamp in the sky who will approve any sinful desire that we consider to be natural. A better metaphor is to view God as the Great Surgeon, with the caveat that God is not interested in mere cosmetic surgery. God is interested in deep-tissue heart surgery.[10]

Here is the fourth truth: *The church's task is to oppose all sin while reaching out in love to all sinners.*

The church should help build a society that neither persecutes the homosexual person nor promotes homosexual behavior. We should oppose any attempt to make "sexual orientation" a specially protected class, or to grant to same-sex relationships the status and benefits comparable to marriage, or to ordain practicing homosexuals as clergy. Our task is always to oppose sin but to reach out in love to sinners.

In John 8 the story is told of a woman caught in the act of adultery. Judgmental religious leaders brought her to Jesus. They wanted our Lord to affirm the penalty required by Mosaic Law, that she be stoned to death. Jesus said, "Let him who is without sin cast the first stone." One by one, starting with the oldest, the religious leaders drifted away. Then Jesus said to the woman, "I do not condemn you. Go and sin no more" (John 8:3–11).

At times the church has thrown rocks at homosexuals rather than to offer help. The church's reputation has been harmed by extremists, such as the Reverend Fred Phelps of Kansas City, who call homosexuals crude, hurtful names. Some of the rest of us have ridiculed them privately, told jokes about them, or have regarded them with hostile apathy. We must repent for our unloving attitudes toward homosexual persons.

That brings me to the final truth: *If a sinner cannot see and feel the love of Jesus in us, our witness is not Christian.*

People practicing homosexuality are not the church's enemies. They are simply people in need of the church's love and support in order to restore to wholeness their broken sexuality.

We must speak the truth to these persons, but always, as St. Paul reminds us, "speaking the truth in love" (Ephesians 4:15).

We must do more than require homosexuals to be celibate. We must include these persons in our fellowship, treasuring them as brothers and sisters, praying with them and for them, and letting them be part of our mutual struggle to grow up into Christ. All of us have a long way to go. We must offer hope and help to people who practice homosexuality. Exodus International is a responsible Christian organization that is active in most American cities, liberating persons from homosexuality.

Let me tell you about John and Anna Paulk. John was formerly a male prostitute and female impersonator. In his book *Every Student's Choice,* he wrote, "In my past there were many masks I hid behind to protect myself." John is now married to Anna, a former lesbian with a similar story. It was her underlying need for love and acceptance that drove her into lesbianism, she says, until Christian friends reached out to her with genuine friendship.

John and Anna are quick to talk about the transforming power of God in their lives. The good news of Christ's love brought them out of homosexuality. John said, "The Lord's transforming power was so evident during our wedding that my mother and stepfather prayed to receive Christ that night."[11]

The truth that homosexual activists will not accept is that thousands upon thousands of individuals have successfully left the homosexual lifestyle. According to Bill Consiglio, director of Hope Ministries, forty percent of homosexuals who seek change move to full heterosexuals, with many entering marriage and parenthood. An additional forty percent are able to live fulfilling lives as celibate Christian singles.[12]

God *accepts* us as we are, but he loves us too much to *leave* us as we are.

Hugh Downs interviewed Billy Graham on the *20/20* television program. The subject turned to homosexuality. Hugh looked directly at Billy and asked, "If you had a homosexual child, would you love him?" Instantly Billy replied, "Why, I would love that one even more."

ENDNOTES

[1] William J. Bennett, *The Broken Hearth* (New York: Broadway Books, 2001), 105.

[2] Bennett, op. cit., 106.

[3] Ibid., 125.

[4] Robert A. J. Gagnon, *The Bible and Homosexual Practice* (Nashville: Abingdon, 2001), 487.

[5] Chuck Colson, *Answers to Your Kids' Questions* (Wheaton: Tyndale, 2000), 115.

[6] Ibid., 117.

[7] H. Newton Malony, "Homosexuality in the Postmodern World," in *Staying the Course,* eds. Maxie D. Dunnam and H. Newton Malony (Nashville: Abingdon, 2003), 131.

[8] J. E. Allen, "Health Agenda Focuses Attention on Gay's Needs," *The Los Angeles Times,* April 30, 2001, Sec. S, 1, 5.

[9] Malony, op. cit., 132.

[10] Robert A. J. Gagnon, "The Bible and Homosexual Practice: Theology, Analogies, and Genes," *Theology Matters,* vol. 7, no. 6, Nov/Dec 2001, 2.

[11] Colson, op. cit., 116.

[12] Ibid., 117.

QUESTIONS

1. List real life, practical examples of ways we can oppose sin, such as homosexuality, but love sinners.
2. Why has homosexuality, once an unmentionable topic, become so socially acceptable so quickly in recent years?
3. Many people assert that homosexuality is genetically determined, and therefore must be God's will. At the very least, the argument goes, people should not be forbidden to follow their natural inclinations. From a biblical perspective, what are the errors in this line of reasoning?
4. Do you agree with the author when he says homosexual orientation is *not* a sin? Why or why not?
5. Are negative effects of homosexual behavior, such as homosexuals' higher suicide rate, the natural consequences of sinful behavior, or are they caused by society's lack of acceptance of homosexuality, as some would argue?
6. Homosexuals contend that God loves them just the way they are, and we know from the Bible that is true. So why can't we agree to allow homosexual marriage?
7. Why do homosexual activists deny the fact that thousands of individuals have left the homosexual lifestyle?
8. Why must we repent of any unloving attitudes toward homosexual persons?